The Buddha Meets Socrates
a philosopher's journal

Harrison J. Pemberton

Series

Bird
of
Paradise
Press

ABOUT BIRD OF PARADISE PRESS

Bird of Paradise Press is a non-profit book publisher based in the United States. The press specializes in Buddhist meditation and philosophy, as well as other topics from Buddhist perspectives including history, ethics, and governance. Its books are distributed worldwide and available in multiple languages. The bird mentioned in the company's name is said to be from a special place where beings can meet with favorable conditions to progress on their path to awakening.

The Buddha Meets Socrates
a philosopher's journal

Harrison J. Pemberton

RABSEL
PUBLICATIONS

Rabsel Publications
16, rue de Babylone
76430 La Remuée, France
www.rabsel.com
contact@rabsel.com

This project was supported by the DRAC and Normandy Region under the FADEL
Normandie, France.

© Rabsel Publications, La Remuée, France, 2022
ISBN: 978-2-36017-033-3

Dedicated with admiration and appreciation
to His Holiness Trinley Thaye Dorje.

Contents

Acknowledgments

I wish to thank Shamar Rinpoche for initiating the writing of this book by inviting me to the Advanced School of Buddhism in Kalimpong to meet with the Karmapa. As the journal will show, the young Karmapa could well be listed as co-author, for as in genuine dialogue two minds are equally at work. I thank him most heartily for our stimulating and enlightening time together.

I wish also to thank Erik Curren, who was and is a most helpful companion in these endeavors, Jachi Shiu for her photographs and for her intelligent insights, and Derek Hanger, who kindly showed me the way in Kalimpong. Also, thanks to Khenpo Tsering Samdup, the principal of the monks' school, for many favors, to all the bright young monks I had the pleasure to teach, and the school staff who gave me every assistance.

My thanks go to Annie Heckman for her new design of this edition, and to Jacqueline U. Heckman and Philip E. Heckman for their assistance with editing this manuscript.

Introduction

Kalimpong

In many a book about India, in the first sentence there is some description of the well-nigh overwhelming onslaught of impressions, the astonishing contrasts, the sheer density of people, the shabbiness and the beauty, the squalor and the magnificence, the turmoil and the tranquility; and obviously this first sentence is no exception.

The locus of this account of a meeting of East and West is the city of Kalimpong in West Bengal, the Darjeeling District, in northeastern India. It is just south of Sikkim and the lofty Himalayas. On a ridge four thousand feet high, and on a parallel just south of Florida, Kalimpong is never too cold and being so high never too hot. As we saw on the trip up to Kalimpong from the train station down in Siliguri, the scenery is alpine but with tropical lushness complete with banana trees, wild orchids, bamboo more than one hundred feet high, and haughty monkeys beside the road ready to pick up any edible trash motorists may toss out. It is said that people live a long time here. Shangri-La?

Kalimpong during Monsoon. Photo by the author.

Hardly. The town is shockingly grungy by our standards, the streets ragged and little more than a rough surface surrounding holes, the traffic a fluid congestion accompanied by incessant horn-blowing, the small shops shabby and much in need of fresh paint, hundreds of dogs completely indifferent to human beings and vice versa, all seen, as we arrived, in a drenching monsoon that should have ended weeks earlier than our October arrival. Not an endearing beginning.

As the monsoon finally rained itself out, however, and as we came to know the town better, the picture changed. The cars and trucks are driven by professional drivers, and though to an American driver who is uncomfortable if another vehicle or pedestrian is closer than three feet, here they pass one another with a comfortable three or four inches. Fender-benders are extremely rare, and there is no evidence of road rage. It is quite amazing and takes some getting used to. The shops, shabby as they may be on the outside, are neat and clean on the inside, with a friendly person ready to help—and to bargain. All in all, Kalimpong works. Never mind that there are frequent power outages; after a while the lights come on again.

In New Delhi, three days before we reached Kalimpong, Pasang, the director of the school where we would stay, spotted us late at night in the crowd at the airport. What a pleasure it is to be met by a friendly and helpful person in a busy and confusing airport half way around the world! He took us to the Karmapa International Buddhist Institute where we could enjoy some much needed rest. The next day he showed us around Delhi and arranged our train tickets. The following day, he took us to the train, indeed, to our very compartment. Moreover, he called ahead so that when we arrived in Siliguri after our twenty-four hour train ride two monks in red robes came to our compartment, took our bags, and ushered us to a shiny SUV for the two hour trip up the mountain to Kalimpong.

Erik Curren and I came here in the fall of 2004 at the invitation of Shamar Rinpoche, the highest-ranking lama under the Karmapa, the spiritual leader of the Karma Kagyu school of Tibetan Buddhism. I knew Erik as a student when I was teaching at Washington and Lee University in Virginia in the mid-eighties. After he graduated, he went on to earn his Ph.D. in English at the University of California, Irvine, only to move into a bleak job market. After several teaching posts, one in Czechoslovakia, he saw brighter possibilities in the business world and then in lobbying work for environmental causes in Washington, all the while becoming more and more interested in Buddhism—so much so that he gave himself a couple of years' retreat at the Bodhi Path Buddhist Center in Virginia, just south of where I live in Lexington. There, I met with him after a hiatus of some twenty years.

When Shamar Rinpoche made one of his periodic visits to the center, which he founded in 1998, the three of us were talking, and after some philosophical reference Shamar Rinpoche said rather casually, "Oh, I know so little about Western philosophy and the monks at the school know even less." Then, he turned to me and said, "Why don't you come to India and teach us Western philosophy?" I wanted to blurt out, "Say when!" but probably said something more casual but still affirmative. That was in the fall of 2003, and I knew by the end of that academic year I would retire after teaching philosophy at Washington and Lee for forty-two years. I was already wondering if I had made the right decision to give up teaching, so the suggestion was exciting. Teaching Buddhist monks in India? I hardly knew what to think, but I was indeed attracted.

In the spring, Shamar Rinpoche decided that October would be the best time for me to come to Asia; and moreover he said that Erik could come also, for he could help him on other projects. Erik remarked that because we would be going in October I would have the whole summer to read up on Buddhism, and Shamar Rinpoche made a curious remark. He said "Oh no, don't do that. The monks must adjust to you, not you to them." I thought about that often as I diligently read up on Buddhism during the summer.

I was most pleased that Erik could come with me; for though I had been to India briefly thirty-two years earlier, Erik had been to Kalimpong recently and would be a most welcome guide and companion.

There was a more important purpose for these plans. I was to teach Buddhist monks, yes, but one in particular who stands out in every way, His Holiness the 17th Gyalwa Karmapa, Trinley Thaye Dorje. Then twenty-one years old, he has been poised to be more and more prominent as the Karmapa in the international scene as well as in India and neighboring predominantly Buddhist countries—Nepal, Bhutan, and Tibet. The responsibility he takes on is enormous, and he is preparing himself assiduously. I was deeply honored and privileged to be one of his teachers and, as I found out very quickly, I was pedagogically rewarded, for the young Karmapa is intellectually very strong indeed. As we shall see, he is both firmly founded in Buddhism and confidently open-minded. Moreover, he speaks English fluently. I could not imagine a more rewarding opportunity after my retirement.

For the reader no more informed than I was at the time, let me add here some words on Tibetan Buddhism. There are four major lineages or schools each with its spiritual head. The Dalai Lama is a leader in the Gelug school; the older Karma Kagyu school speaks of its head as the Karmapa, and there are two others, the Nyingma, and the Sakya schools. The Dalai Lama is not the head of the other lineages any more than the Pope is of the Protestant denominations, but he, like the Pope, is the most prominent on the international scene.

The young Karmapa is the spiritual head of the Karma Kagyu school, but Shamar Rinpoche, first in rank under the Karmapa, is the main administrator. He oversees numerous Buddhist centers all over the world, and he does it all with great efficiency and good humor as though it were easy. When the 16th Karmapa died in 1981, it fell to Shamar Rinpoche as the top-ranking lama to recognize the reincarnated next Karmapa. This he did. He recognized the young Karmapa, Trinley Thaye Dorje, when he was eleven years old, and he has since supervised his education, all the while administering the elaborate Karma Kagyu school.

Wednesday market in Kalimpong. Photo by the author.

There has been, however, serious controversy. Situ Rinpoche, third in rank under the Karmapa, working outside the traditional procedure but with the support of the Chinese government in Tibet, recognized another boy as the 17th Karmapa, Orgyen Trinley. The Dalai Lama, though in another school, the Gelug school, but perhaps in an attempt to improve relations with the Chinese, gave his support to their candidate; and with his enormous prestige has made Orgyen Trinley prominent in the media. Several books have been published that argue in favor of Ogyen Trinley or just assume his priority. With judicious scholarship and thoroughness, Erik Curren has explored the tangled complications of this affair in his book, *Buddha's Not Smiling: Uncovering Corruption at the Heart of Tibetan Buddhism Today*. Unfortunately, this controversy continues, but there is hope that in time there will be a peaceful resolution in the Buddhist manner. The young Karmapa regards all this with admirable realism and calm. Because my concerns were strictly pedagogical and philosophical, these complications were set aside and did not enter our discussions at all.

Shamar Rinpoche provided a small house near the school for Erik and me, and as we were moving in a young man helped us and announced that he was to be our cook. Our young cook, Dawa, was from Bhutan and had been serving the Karmapa's parents. Because they were away, he came to us. He is a very good-natured young man, pleasant to have about, and a splendid cook. We were treated well in Kalimpong!

The rain let up a bit the next day when we were to meet the Karmapa. Dawa brought us two diaphanous silk scarves, one white, one yellow, and showed us the proper way to greet the Karmapa and then offer the scarves. In the misty morning light that allowed us to see the mountains for the first time we followed Dawa down the path to the Karmapa's house next to the school. There we were met by the secretary to the Karmapa, Karma Deng, another very cheerful and efficient young man from Bhutan. He took us to a plain but comfortable waiting room, and Dawa and an older monk carefully rolled up the scarves and returned them to us.

After a few minutes Karma Deng led us to the door of another room where we removed our shoes. We entered the room to greet His Holiness. He sat on a dark blue chair just a little broader than the usual Western upholstered chair, looked up with a pleasant and friendly smile and seemed just slightly bemused by these Americans.

We exchanged greetings, and then Erik and I presented him the two rolled-up scarves. Somehow I conveyed that I felt a bit awkward, for with a gentle gesture and smile he indicated that he was not a stickler for ceremony on such an occasion. He blessed the scarves, unrolled them, and then as we bowed he draped them around our necks. Then, he gave each of us a small red ribbon to protect us from any dangers that might emerge from within ourselves. So much for ceremony.

We sat on cushions and after some conventional comments on the weather—he wondered if global warming had anything to do with the extended monsoon—we spoke briefly of the reasons for our being there, and he expressed his pleasure in having us with him. He spoke softly in perfect English. When there was a brief silence, we took it that our audience was over, and we left with polite words all around.

As we left the house, both Erik and I remarked on how mature and self-assured the young Karmapa had become. We had seen a DVD showing him on his eighteenth birthday; he was in full teenage bloom, handsome, lively, laughing, and endearing as the young can be. Now at twenty-one his face had become more masculine, stronger, his manner self-controlled and at ease. More important for my purposes was his obvious intelligence and good will.

Karma Deng then took us next door to the monks' college or shedra, the Institute for Advanced Buddhist Studies, to meet the principal, Khenpo Tsering Samdup.

Here again was a most pleasant man who administers a complex organization as though it were easy. He made us feel quite welcome and took us around to see the school. The monks, usually about sixty, live on the first floor, classrooms are on the second, and on the third is the beautiful shrine. Unlike the other Buddhist shrines I had seen in which the colors are intense, so much so that one feels hesitant to enter, this one was designed by Shamar Rinpoche and had softer, cheerful pastels, and one felt comfortably drawn in. There are courtyards around the building and a dining hall and apartments beyond. The monks' world is pleasantly self-contained, a monastery but a place for easy smiles.

Khenpo Tsering arranged for the class to meet for five weeks, five days a week at two o'clock, and after each class I would meet privately with the Karmapa for an hour. The Khenpo thought there would be some thirty monks in the class. There were, but after a class or two only seven monks thought their English, or their interest, was sufficient to continue. Erik volunteered to meet with the others in a class for conversational English, so it all worked out.

The Khenpo was helpful and accommodating throughout our stay. We noticed that the chalk boards in the classrooms were severely worn, and Erik suggested that we offer to buy new white boards for the school. The Khenpo immediately had two new boards made, but he would not hear of our paying for them.

Sometime later in one of our conferences, His Holiness explained that unlike yogis in other lineages who go directly to meditation with few preliminaries, in a cave perhaps, in Tibetan Buddhism there are lengthy preliminaries. First, as at the shedra, there is intense study of Buddhist texts; second, there is assimilation and contemplation; then third, meditation. At the shedra he said they are mainly at the first stage. His Holiness often remarked that he was still a student.

My challenge was to introduce Western philosophy to well-educated Buddhist monks in five weeks. Introducing philosophy to American students who are also well-prepared is challenge enough, as I know from years of experience. At least language was not an issue with those American students, and I could work with certain expectations for their schooling in mathematics, Western history, literature, science, and the other disciplines that shape Western culture. In Kalimpong, language was indeed a problem, except for in my meetings with the Karmapa, and I could not draw on, as we say, what every schoolboy knows. The history and major figures in the West were virtually unknown to the monks, and the philosophical endeavor I hoped to bring them into, and the Socratic pedagogy needed to generate that endeavor, were so foreign to them that to the present day I do not know what success I had.

In 1971 I held a seminar at Chung Chi College in the Chinese University of Hong Kong, and there, as at home, language was not a problem; but even though some had schooling in the British pattern, the Confucian culture that shaped them brought its own challenge. There were twelve students in the seminar, but try as I may I could not get them to engage in the sort of exchange typical in a seminar in American colleges. As they told me, their training had been to revere the teacher as though he were perched high on a pedestal while they dutifully absorbed what he had to say, holding their own thoughts back. One student did presume to make a comment in the seminar, and afterward he was reprimanded by another student. She said, "We did not come here to hear what you have to say, but what the teacher has to say." After class with several of the students at a round table in the dining hall, the talk was lively and invigorating, and I thought an opening had been made; but during the next class they sat quietly, pencils in hand, ready to record the words of the teacher. I expected a similar obstacle in India. Rightly so, as I have just indicated.

There were further challenges. I was to introduce Western philosophy but without the slightest intention of shifting them from the Buddhist thought they were so avidly studying. Rather I hoped to show the monks other ways of thinking that could not only show the merit of Western thought but also provide a contrast that would allow them to see their own Buddhist thinking all the more clearly. This could also have advantages later on as these monks, once they become teachers, could have an assignment in the West. The Karmapa certainly will have more and more dealings in the West.

It works the other way also. After my time in Kalimpong, I came to see our own Western way of thought all the more clearly in its contrast with Buddhism. In what follows, that contrast will be a major theme, but beyond it, perplexing questions emerge about the purpose of philosophical endeavors in general. Why engage in philosophical inquiries at all? Or, as every student majoring in philosophy often hears, "What can you do with philosophy?" The snappy rejoinder that the question should be "What can philosophy do with you?" has its point just as a response, but it can also lead to some very serious reflections. If a Buddhist were asked such a question, he could answer quite simply that the Buddha can show you a way out of suffering and lead you to an ultimate peace and happiness. Being a religion as well as a philosophy, Buddhism addresses the way we can live our lives.

The author, seated with His Holiness the 17th Karmapa Trinley Thaye Dorje. Photo by Jachi Shiu.

In contrast, Western philosophy is more and more an academic discipline, perhaps enticing enough to lead a student into an academic career (or at the level of the original question, a good way to get into law school), but the immediate and unavoidable questions of life and death are left to religion—or just left to happenstance. Even courses in ethics, though they may clarify the concepts involved, do not show, or even intend to show, how we should live our lives. I recall the opening sentence of a visiting professor fresh from Cambridge in a graduate seminar on ethics: "Moral philosophy has nothing to do with human behavior." Then what does? Socrates, Plato, Aristotle, and the subsequent Hellenistic philosophers make it clear why the philosophical life is the good life, but currently philosophy is kept comfortably within academe where it may offer some conceptual clarity; after that it is up to the student to make the most of it. This academic confinement is all the more clear in contrast with Buddhism, especially in a monastery where Buddhism is the life of the monks.

There is, however, strength in the Western way of education that needs to be recognized. Philosophy may be confined as just one among the many disciplines in our colleges and universities, but in the larger context of the institution the overall effect is philosophic in a broader sense, and philosophic in the Western mode. In facing the contingencies and challenges of life we realize we do not know all the answers and that in order to see the best way to proceed we must rely on the strength of disciplined reason and an open mind that can see opportunities. Such a basis for life is exactly what a liberal education hopes to provide. The students take courses not only in philosophy but also in mathematics, literature, history, the sciences, and art. The net effect is a developed intellect and a broadened vision. The students gain a keener sense of intellectual problems and a developed intellect to attempt to deal with them. In short, they acquire a philosophic basis for their lives. Philosophy is an ongoing endeavor, or as the Greeks have it, the love of wisdom or, more specifically, the love of intellectual clarity; and that orientation and dedication is the basis of the good life, or, for some of the major Greek thinkers, it is the good life. It is easy to imagine the ghost of Socrates smiling, for his wisdom was that he knew he did not know and that careful inquiry was the best human response. Or more dramatically in the Greek mode, we are thrust into life in ignorance and must accept the need to inquire. It is our fate. In Western institutions of higher learning that is the heart of the matter: an awareness of new problems, disciplined inquiry, and careful innovation. In short: a vigorous, ongoing intellectual activity.

My remark above that the students are left to make the most of their education can then have a positive interpretation, for with a developed reason and an open mind students can indeed make the most of their lives. We will see how this Western way of education, that may seem too familiar to readers in the West to need explication, will be seen all the more clearly in contrast with an Eastern way.

Throughout the centuries many people have made a journey to India on a spiritual quest, drawn by its ancient culture, religion, and philosophy. But I do not fit the pattern. I was there to show a few Buddhists another way of thinking, and what I would gain by that endeavor in faraway India was secondary. Even so, it was a rich and rewarding experience, a provocation for much wonder. More on wonder later.

In anticipating my journey to the monastery, I thought it most likely that I would learn more than the students in my time there. That is one of the secrets of academe, for it is in the challenge to present ideas clearly and respond to questions that a teacher can come to see the issues with more and more clarity. That is the usual case, but in the school in Kalimpong it was considerably more of a learning experience, for after class in discussion with His Holiness, I encouraged him more and more to express the Buddhist view of the issues because I had spent time in class presenting the Western positions. The roles of teacher and student became blurred in a very rewarding way. I hope this becomes clear in what follows.

I thought the most appropriate beginning would be to introduce them to Socrates and see if he could enthrall them as he did young Athenians who most likely had been captivated by skillful sophists. Clearly, Plato's *Meno* was the suitable introduction. After that I planned to look at the central part of the *Republic* to show the monks the larger Platonic position. Then, we would take a giant step to modern philosophy and a consideration of Descartes and, by extension, modern science, then on to Hume who has significant compatibilities with Buddhist thought. Erik urged me to address the curious disregard of history in Indian thought, so with some trepidation I planned a consideration of Hegel and Marx. Finally, I wanted to emphasize the ongoing nature of Western philosophy and the possibility of an opening to Eastern thought. In one quite accessible address to a general audience, Heidegger opens that possibility, so we would conclude with that.

Jachi Shiu, a friend of Erik and an expert photographer, joined us in mid-term, to make photographs of the Karmapa, the other monks, and our involvement with them. After our stay in Kalimpong the three of us made our way to Bodh Gaya. There, like so many pilgrims, we sat under the tree thought to be from a sprout of the tree the Buddha sat beneath when he attained enlightenment twenty-five hundred years ago. The tree, some hundred years old, stands just west of the towering Mahabodhi temple. Its trunk is enclosed by an ornate stone fence while its limbs and leaves spread out across a larger fenced-in area where pilgrims can sit. It was a clean and peaceful place; some Thai monks in saffron robes sat in a row softly chanting, a few devotees passed by, one taking two steps then making a prostration and so on all around the temple; and bright-eyed children ran here and there but quietly. We sat there silently for a while; then, although it was not the time for leaves to fall, one did fall right in front of me. I picked it up to keep but resisted, not quite successfully, taking it as a good omen.

chapter 1
Can virtue be taught?

After many years of teaching I had lost some of the excitement that young instructors feel when meeting a class for the first time, but here in Kalimpong halfway around the world from home the excitement welled up again. The students were monks in red robes, hair cut very short, with smiling faces. I was something of an oddity, non- Asian, white-haired and speaking a language they had studied but had little experience of hearing from a native speaker. This excitement and strangeness was complemented by an evident cordiality and respect, and though I was feeling as excited as a young instructor, I felt quite comfortable launching into what I had planned for my introductory remarks.

There were two major themes that I hoped would order the whole course. The first may be called pedagogical, for we are concerned at the start with two most notable teachers, the Buddha and Socrates.

Notable teachers start by working with the ignorance or ordinary opinion of their students, then try by some technique to move them to a higher or deeper insight or understanding. But even in this basic description of teaching, we see a major difference that defines our first theme. Generally, in traditional Western philosophy, it is by the exercise of disciplined reason that one hopes to attain intellectual clarity; in traditional Eastern thought it is by well-practiced meditation that one hopes to attain enlightenment. I put forth this contrast as a working hypothesis, and it will indeed help us order many of the ideas and problems we want to consider, but this scheme needs much elaboration, and possibly qualification, and correction. Even here at the outset we should notice that putting forth this theme is itself an attempt to move toward intellectual clarity. Or is it? Let this question hover over our discussion: From what viewpoint can one see the contrast of Eastern and Western modes of thought?

The second theme I hoped to explore was the nature of time: in simplest terms, the linear time we take for granted and the cyclical time Buddhists take for granted.

We can get further into our first major theme by noticing what to some is a curious claim that both the Buddha and Socrates make. Both claim that their pedagogy attempts to bring to the fore what is already there in the aspirant or student. Socrates claims that knowledge is recollection and does not come by gathering a great deal of information; in effect his pedagogy is to lead us from mere opinion to what by reason we can recognize as intelligible. Similarly, the Buddha would show us the way back to the timeless light of our true mind that we have obscured in this ordinary life.

In the dialogue *Theaetetus*, Plato has Socrates make fun of an ordinary opinion of teaching, a way of picturing the mind as a birdcage into which a teacher may insert pieces of knowledge like so many birds. Both the Buddha and Socrates appeal to our true nature, what we are and have been all along, who we are at the deepest level; rather than adding anything, like pieces of knowledge, they would dispel something, the obscurations and distractions.

This similarity, however, immediately opens into a difference (a turn we will see time and time again), for what the Buddha means by the mind's true nature is radically different from what Socrates would see as its true nature.

This bears directly on the topic of our first reading to be considered at the next class, Plato's *Meno*.[1] In that dialogue Meno swaggers up to Socrates and asks him, "Can virtue be taught?" Socrates, with more acidic irony than usual, says he does not know, for he does not even know what virtue is, and so he asks Meno to tell him. The critical word here is *arete*, which we usually translate as "virtue," sometimes as "excellence," and I wanted to convey something of what the Greeks meant by that word as introduction to the dialogue.

I used the example of the knife: any knife, as a knife, has a blade that will at least cut butter, but to cut well it needs its particular virtue, sharpness, the condition it must be in to function well. The Karmapa saw this immediately while the others, with eye-brows up and together, seemed puzzled. After a few more examples they could see that a virtue is the condition of something

---

1   *Meno* 82 d-e, W.R.M. Lamb trans, Loeb Classical Library, Harvard University Press, Cambridge, Massachusetts, 1962

working well, and for human beings that means being in such a condition that we can live well, i.e. be happy. Just as an athlete needs to have his body in good condition in order to compete well, so the whole human being, especially the mind, needs to be in good condition in order to live well. But then, what is that condition? That is what Socrates hopes to help us understand.

The Karmapa then asked, "Isn't that rather selfish?" I immediately took that as an opportunity to expound more of Plato's thought and so gave a hasty sketch of the necessity of the fully virtuous person to play his or her role in the community; that is, the virtuous person would not be selfish but would be concerned with the good for all in the community. The Karmapa did not seem pleased but did not object. It was only later in discussion with him that I realized I had missed the purport of his question. He had another meaning of selfish in mind, not selfish as being concerned only with one's own advantage, but rather selfish in the sense of being so involved with mundane concerns and one's individual ego that one is distracted from the non-individual Buddha nature, the union of wisdom and compassion understood as the true nature of all sentient beings. From this perspective, any clinging to the idea of a stably existing self is selfish. Being so concerned with the individual ego, we have obscured the true self, and from that point of view Greek arête does seem focused on individual virtue even if that involves a social awareness. Human virtue, the best condition one can be in, in the Buddhist sense, would be enlightenment. Something of the Greek notion that virtue is the condition of functioning well may still hold, but because for the Buddhist that condition is one of the selflessness of the Buddha nature, the Greek pattern is radically altered. The Karmapa's question is then very much to the point.

After the first class, which quite a number of monks attended, we moved to a smaller room because only seven monks from the original group thought their understanding of English was sufficient to continue. In that smaller room there was only one chair for me, and the monks sat on a nicely figured oriental rug on the floor. But before the Karmapa arrived, two monks hastily found another chair for him to sit in. This he did at first, but after the second class he sat on the rug with the other monks. When I told Shamar Rinpoche of this he said, "Good for him, good for him."

Monks in class. Photo by the author.

In a later class, when due to illness the Karmapa was not present, I wanted to try harder to elicit responses from the monks, and without thinking I sat down on the rug close to them. They all burst out laughing. I had done something so ludicrous they could not hold back. So I sat on the chair while they sat at my feet. Not my style at all! Finally, I stood at the board and went on as though with a large class hoping my diagrams would elicit some questions. None were forthcoming. I recalled that the Chinese students in Hong Kong could not bring themselves to ask questions because, as one explained it to me, they thought that would be rude, as though saying that the teacher had failed in his effort to be clear, that he is a poor teacher. It turned out that the monks shared this idea of their relation to the teacher.

To entice the monks into some of the dynamics of the *Meno* I gave them a neat geometric puzzle to play with over the weekend. In the critical central part of the dialogue Socrates poses a geometrical problem to one of Meno's slaves to show Meno how he should proceed. I hoped a neat geometrical puzzle would help the monks see the point that Meno missed: Take six toothpicks or matches all the same length and construct four equilateral triangles each side of which is the length of the toothpick or match. Or, I said, they could draw the figure on a piece of paper. In my experience only two or three students in a class of twenty-five or so work it out, so predictably of my seven students only one got it. His Holiness brought to class the next time the completed figure he had constructed of matches. He told me as soon as I gave the problem he pictured in his mind how to solve it. This did not surprise me, because he told me that as a child he enjoyed fixing the complicated toys of his younger brother, and someone in his household told me that when a computer stopped working, the Karmapa could take it apart and fix it. He is clearly adept with spatial configurations. I asked him to hide his construction and then play the role of Socrates with one of the monks who had not yet worked it out.

In the *Meno*, Plato gives us the model. Socrates drew in the sand a square with two units on each side to yield an area of four and asked a slave boy in service to Meno how he could draw a square of double that, a square with the area of eight. Notice how crafty Socrates proceeds. Referring to the square of eight, he says, "Come now, try and tell me how long will each side of that figure be. This one is two feet long, what will be the side of the other, which is double in size?" The boy immediately said double the side of the square of four, but when Socrates drew the figure in the sand the boy could see that gave a square of sixteen; he tried three, but that gave an area of nine. The boy was perplexed, stymied; as the Greeks had it, he was in a state of aporia (inability to go through). As well he might be, for as mathematicians can show, the slave boy could go on guessing forever, because the side of the square is the square root of eight, an irrational number. i.e., it cannot be expressed as the product of two whole numbers. My calculator tells me it is 2.82871 ... indefinitely. Socrates deliberately led the boy into that impasse to bring him to realize he did not know but also to trigger his desire to know.

It was then that Socrates shifted the boy's attention to the diagonal, and once he could see how drawing the diagonal through the four squares of an area of four each inside the square of sixteen, cutting each in half, the result would be a square of eight. The boy then saw clearly that the double of a square is constructed on the diagonal.

Though Plato does not have him say it, I wish the boy had said "Ah ha!"

Playing his role in class and following the Socratic pattern, His Holiness then asked the perplexed monk precisely the apt question, the question that could trigger his insight into the solution. In Socratic fashion I had misled the monks by suggesting they draw the figure on a piece of paper, knowing that no two dimensional arrangement of the sticks or lines could work. Accordingly, His Holiness asked him if he assumed that the figure had to be a flat figure, and with a rephrasing in Tibetan (that I could not understand, of course) the monk after a try or two pulled three matches up from a triangle constructed on the desk to make a point above and thus made the tetrahedron. The monk did not say "Ah ha!" either, but I hoped there was some appreciation of the sudden clarity and certainty reason can attain in mathematics.

What Plato would have us see is that the capacity for rational insight that the slave boy showed is, when developed, the essential human virtue and the basis of the other virtues. That is what Meno needed to see, but did not. When Socrates asked Meno to say what virtue is, he thought it would be easy and offered several hasty definitions, but none stood up to Socrates' criticisms. Finally, Meno recalled something he had heard before and said, virtue is the power to attain good. Socrates thought that might be right, but when he asked Meno to explain what his definition meant he failed again and became not only perplexed but angry. He brought up a quibble to the effect that inquiry is pointless.

To bring Meno around again Socrates told him a strange story he had heard from priests and priestesses that in a previous life the soul had full knowledge, but now thrust back into the confusions of mundane life the soul is obscured and has the task of recollecting what it had apprehended before. Having just said inquiry is pointless Meno is curious and asks Socrates to explain. To show that knowledge is recollection Socrates questioned the slave boy. What Meno should have seen is that his slave followed a procedure like his own: first he was confident he knew, Socrates shows him he does not, he is stymied, and then when Socrates redirects his attention, the boy sees clearly what he had, as it were, forgotten. When Meno was stymied Socrates hoped to redirect his attention to the power the slave boy shows in solving his problem, the power to come to a clarity and certainty in sharp contrast to his opinions and guessing before. Meno should have seen that this capacity the slave boy showed is the power to attain good that he could not make clear before. I still wonder if the monks other than the Karmapa saw the point. They told me that they had never studied geometry or much mathematics at all, and it seemed doubtful that seeing the solution to two simple problems would open up a new world of understanding.

Now I was stymied. At the entrance to Plato's Academy it was written "Let No Non-geometer Enter," and here I was trying to introduce non-geometers to Plato. We have spoken of that rational insight that the Meno brings to the fore as intellectual clarity to compare with Buddhist enlightenment, but so far the Western half of our scheme was weak. But then there was a stroke of luck.

At seven-thirty in the morning, before Erik and I had breakfast, there was a loud knock at the door. It was Lama Belu who was the driver for Shamar Rinpoche. He told us that Rinpoche wanted us to come to his house right away. On the way through town and the usual congestion we speculated on what the good Rinpoche had in mind, and Erik thought that perhaps because it was the first clear and sunny day after the lingering monsoon Shamar Rinpoche had asked us to come to his place higher on the ridge so we could see the Himalayas. Erik was right. When we arrived we could see, there on the horizon gleaming in dazzling white, was Kanchenjunga (28,208 feet) with her somewhat less towering attendants. It was indeed a beautiful and inspiring sight, the mountain so clear to us after the gloomy monsoon.

During breakfast, with Kanchenjunga still visible through the open French doors of the beautiful dining room, Erik asked Shamar Rinpoche how he would distinguish *sherab* and *yeshe*. Those were new words to me; both, I learned, are translated as "wisdom." Shamar Rinpoche said *sherab* meant clear conceptual knowledge of this or that while *yeshe* is the wisdom of non-conceptual mind, the final enlightenment, the ultimate wisdom. A person with *sherab* is knowledgeable, and he can be clever but often superficial; even so, it is from *sherab* that one may move on to *yeshe*. Later in discussion the Karmapa compared the man of *sherab* to a person looking through a telescope or a microscope who can see clearly some things and hence have a kind of knowledge. He can know many things from a single perspective, but any perspective is limiting. There can be correctness within limits, but *sherab* falls short of the 'vision' without perspective, ultimate truth. It isn't that *sherab* falls short of an all-inclusive bigger picture, because that would just be seeing objects from a wider perspective, but rather *sherab* falls short of perspectiveless, objectless wisdom of enlightenment, *yeshe*.

The good luck was that I had planned to discuss that very day the famous passages in the *Republic* where Plato in three famous similes has Socrates speak of the Idea of Good, the Divided Line showing the four stages of knowledge, and the Allegory of the Cave. I wanted to focus on the third and fourth stages of knowledge illustrated by the Divided Line. There we see a transition from theoretical understanding at the third stage to a hoped for final clarity at the fourth. At the first and lowest stage we perceive only shadows and images of actual things, but from many shadows and images of an actual thing we can move to see the actual thing itself, going from many to one and from the less real to the more real. Then, analogously, for many actual things there can be one concept perhaps in a theory that explains them; so again we can move from many to one and from temporal things to non-temporal concepts. For example, from many round things we can move to one concept of the circle in a theory of geometry. But there are many theories, and sometimes they are in conflict with one another, as we saw in the episode with the slave boy. A square with an area of eight is simple geometrically, but if we try to specify the length of the side arithmetically, we are stymied; the square root of eight is an irrational number. We are urged beyond both geometry and arithmetic, at the third stage, to seek a higher understanding, an idea, that can make intelligible what stymied us at the third stage.

What seemed inviting, but very tenuous, was a possible similarity of the movement from hypotheses to an idea in Plato's example and the movement from *sherab* to *yeshe* in Buddhist thought. When I put these new words on the board the monks brightened up. Before we had used an old and worn blackboard, but then on that day Khenpo Tsering provided us a new white board with colored ink-pens, and everything was clearer, I hoped intellectually as well as visually. The monks were on familiar ground. They could articulate the difference between *sherab* and *yeshe* quite clearly, and they seemed ready to move on.

Kangchenjunga (28, 208 feet). Photo by Justin Mygatt.

Westerners frequently regard Eastern thought as vague, mystical, or in any case slack on logic, but this notion is far from the truth. Among the exercises the monks engage in is debate, and this is a lively, game-like activity in small groups in which one monk fires questions to another with a sort of sliding hand slap as though sending a missile toward him. The slightest lapse into inconsistency by the questioned monk is immediately noticed and exposed with a vigorous raised hand gesture much to the chagrin of the lapsing monk. The question may be, "Are all things impermanent?" or "Do all beings have Buddha nature?" and the questioned monk must respond quickly but very, very carefully. In responding to the sharp questions, the monk must not only draw on what he has learned and repeat a correct answer, but also he should be opened to deeper meanings he had not quite apprehended. It is a test but also a learning experience. All this is conducted seriously but with high spirits and some laughter. Moreover, in the texts the monks study there is the highest regard for logical consistency. Indeed the rules and forms of logic that great teachers, the lamas, have elaborated would impress even Aristotle.

Moreover, the logical subtlety of their critical engagements with their peers is impressive and challenging. For example, there is the notion of twofold truth, the conventional or relative truth we may have of things in this world versus the ultimate truth of the Buddha mind. But then it is clear that this distinction itself is, after all, conventional. Where does that leave us? The dexterity they show in such discussions would impress scholastics of the middle ages and epistemologists of our day.

Even so what I found missing is the notion of a deductively formulated theory that Plato has at the third stage of knowledge. We are familiar with such a formulation in Euclid's geometry that, though written a short time later, is precisely to the pattern at the third stage. We start with explicit assumptions then step by step draw what can follow logically from them, i.e., as Plato says, we work down from the first assumptions to prove a theorem. The many theorems that can be proved in geometry, for example, are derived by a deduction down from the few first principles, each step justified in reference to them. This intellectual pyramidal structure with the first principles at the top and the many theorems spreading out beneath encourages the idea of an ultimate first principle by reference to which the many theories themselves find their justification.

Plato hopes such an intellectual assent can give us some glimpse of the idea of good, intellectual lucidity itself, the analogue of the sun. If as Edna St. Vincent

Millay says, "Euclid alone has looked on Beauty bare," then my non-geometers are missing something beautiful. They are also missing what is necessary to understand Plato's move to the fourth stage of knowledge. Such a move, that Plato calls dialectic, starts by questioning basic assumptions of a theory or theories in an attempt to articulate a more adequate theory, one more appropriate to a final coherence.

Monks in debate. Photo by the author.

I thought an example from physics might help. The magnificent physical theory that Isaac Newton put forth has, after some three hundred years of astonishing success, come to grief; it could not explain some phenomena having to do with the measurement of the speed of light. Along comes Einstein. He noted that Newton's theory assumes a three dimensional absolute space and a uniformly flowing absolute time. Einstein rejected these assumptions and posited concepts of relative time and space, and he could thereby explain what Newton could not. The intricacies involved here are not to our purpose. Rather it is the movement of thought we need to see. It is an ongoing attempt to approximate a final clarity about something. Another example: light can be regarded as a wave in one context or as a particle in another, but this enlivens the question, What is light itself? Plato calls that final clarity we hope for an idea, something seen; it is that toward which we strive at the fourth stage of knowledge.

After the regular classes His Holiness and I were able to explore in private sessions a wider range of issues, both Socratic and Buddhist. One was the Socratic claim that one who is suitably dedicated and self-disciplined reaches pure intelligence only at death, and before that, as he has it, he can only practice dying. In a typically provocative manner Socrates says:

"Other people are likely not to be aware that those who pursue philosophy aright study nothing but dying and being dead. Now if this is true, it would be absurd to be eager for nothing but this all their lives, and then to be troubled when that came for which they had all along been eagerly practicing."

That is how in the *Phaedo* Socrates spoke of philosophy and his mission, that activity that tries to rise above the temporal confinement and confusions that come with being embodied and reach toward impersonal, disembodied intelligibility, or, as we say now, objective understanding.[2] It is an ongoing endeavor, and for Socrates a life-long mission.

I wanted to sound this particular Western note early and show how Socrates addressed the lack

---

2   *Phaedo* 64a, Plato with an English Translation, Harold North Fowler trans. Haarvard University Press, Boston Massachusetts, 1938.

of finality that we must accept in life and the need for continual intellectual effort. It is unlikely that a modern scientist would speak of his effort to come to an objective understanding, i.e., one that is impersonal, non-subjective, dispassionate, universally acceptable, as practicing dying—unless he reflected on his effort. Would he grant that in trying to dispel subjectivity he, in effect, tries to think as though disembodied? The possible parallel to the practice of meditation needed only the slightest mention, and His Holiness just smiled.

There was another way to appeal to the monks: to exploit the appearance/reality distinction. The monks are quite familiar with this distinction, and they even go further and see not just appearance but illusion as our usual starting point. An excursion into Plato's Cave was in order. There we see prisoners who are chained so that they can only see a wall upon which flickering shadows of models of people, animals, and implements are cast. The models are held up like puppets in front of a fire behind the puppets and prisoners to cast the shadows. Plato would have an easier time of it today, for a reference to the cinema or television would do. As Socrates says, "Then in every way such prisoners would deem reality to be nothing else than the shadows of the artificial objects."[3]

Someone—clearly we are to imagine Socrates—could turn a prisoner around, show him the models and the fire, and then pull him outside into the sunlight. There the freed prisoner could at first see only shadows and reflections of actual things, but then when his eyes become accustomed to the light he could see actual

---

3   ibid. 515 c

things in sunlight. The Socratic enlightening could continue as indicated in the simile of the divided line, from actual things to theories then on toward a final clarity, ideas.

A Buddhist can say that just as in ordinary life we regard images in a mirror as ephemeral and empty illusions, so in enlightenment we will regard the "realities" of ordinary life as mere illusions. But then once again similarity opens into difference. *Sherab* is much like the theoretical understanding at Plato's third stage, but then the major difference is evident. From theoretical understanding we move via dialectic toward a final clarity, the idea; but from *sherab* we move to *yeshe* which is non-conceptual, and indeed we go beyond any sense of a subject attending an object, intellectual or actual. Whatever similarity we may see between *sherab* and theoretical understanding seems lost in the final insight each mode of thought leads to.

I said *seems* because in further discussions with the Karmapa I could suggest how we may glimpse a possible convergence of Socratic and Buddhist insight in other reflections in the *Phaedo*. As Plato relates it, Socrates, knowing he is to be executed at sundown, argues that he does not fear or dread death, for he is confident the soul is immortal. At death the soul is freed from its imprisonment in the body and attains a timeless lucidity. However, his arguments, if sound, only prove that Soul—pure, timeless, and impersonal intelligence—is immortal. He does not show that each individual soul is thereby immortal. His Holiness immediately saw the parallel: one is immortal insofar as he attains the Buddha mind that is non-individual, eternal and all-pervasive. I asked if the mind then becomes *dharma*, as for Socrates the mind becomes intelligibility, and after a hesitation he concurred. But we also agreed these matters need more consideration.

Later, we did reconsider. When I asked again if the mind in enlightenment becomes dharma, His Holiness winced a bit but agreed at least tentatively with my suggested reformulation: dharma is the pattern of Active Mind. He had already said he prefers to speak of *shunyata*, the ultimate non-conceptual openness, as "active mind" rather than as "emptiness," as it is usually translated. The Karmapa finds the usual translation misleading. Every moment is an ending, no longer there, empty, yes; but every moment is also a beginning, and this endlessly. A wave on the sea is momentary but opens a way for the rise of another wave and so on endlessly, and this dynamic openness, if I understand him, the Karmapa prefers to regard as "active mind" rather than "emptiness." Dharma as the pattern of active mind made Buddhist insights much clearer to me, and I hope it can hold up to expert criticism.

But, no, it doesn't. Dharma is used in the sense of doctrine or law, but more accurately it is spoken of as the way to enlightenment, the cleansing by right living and lengthy meditation that can free the mind to its true nature. But that true nature is without pattern. My suggestion was too Western.

I hoped to explore this further, for it seems to show a way to reply to the question Buddhists so frequently hear, and the one I asked His Holiness: Just what is it that is reincarnated? There is no soul entity that survives death and thence can animate a new body, but then, if not some such entity, just what is reincarnated? His reply was that it is a pattern of mind that is repeated. I could see that this could mean a pattern of thought, speech, and behavior, a personality so to speak, that survives any one person, and thus we avoid the notion of a soul as an entity that goes from one body to another. We can consider this difficult problem again when we take note of David Hume, the 18th century British empiricist, who also rejects any notion of a soul entity.

In contrast but equally difficult to articulate, as we have seen, is what Plato speaks of as fundamental in his thought, the idea of good. Socrates says he cannot say directly what it is but that he can offer an analogy.

As the sun shedding its light is the condition whereby our eyes can see objects in the perceptible realm, so we are to see an analogous three-part scheme in the intelligible and unseen realm. There the idea of good is the condition of the mind apprehending intelligible objects, namely theories and ideas, as the sun is the condition of the eye seeing visible things and their shadows. This image of the idea of good as the very source of things intelligible as an analogue to the sun and its light is quite appealing and has had, needless to say, massive influence in Western philosophy and theology ever since. The idea of good as intelligibility itself was later elaborated into God's wisdom, and it still casts its spell at the naturalistic level and non-theologically as the idea that there is an intelligible explanation for the phenomena of nature, i.e. that there is a possible scientific explanation for any phenomenon we may strive toward. Such an idea motivates scientific research, and in philosophy motivates our efforts to be conceptually clear.

But then with such clarity there comes a problem, indeed a puzzle. If we look directly at the sun we are blinded, and analogously, if we look directly to the idea of good, we are bedazzled. He has Socrates complete the analogy:

You will agree that the Sun not only makes the things we
see visible, but also brings them into existence and gives
them growth and nourishment; yet he [the sun] is not
the same thing as existence. And so with the objects of
knowledge; these derive from the Good not only their
power of being known, but their very being and reality;
and Goodness is not the same thing as being, but even
beyond being surpassing it in dignity and power.[4]

Beyond being? Plato knew when to be vague, and here
he only leaves us with the analogy of the idea of good
we cannot see clearly to the sun that blinds us if we look
at it. Then, where are we? This stretches the intellect
to the limit and apparently beyond. As *yeshe* surpasses
sherab?

His Holiness is stimulated by puzzles and problems
to be faced in dealing with fundamental issues, and
he was a most congenial companion in all these
explorations. We had occasion to discuss again the
argument Socrates offers in the *Phaedo* to show that a
suitably purified soul, when it is disembodied at death,
becomes pure non-individual intellect. Is it then, being
non-individual, beyond the subject-object relation?
Does it attain *shunyata*, openness/active mind? Do
ultimate intellectual clarity and *yeshe* then converge?

The subject-object relation is certainly in question
in another curious topic Plato comes to in a very late
dialogue, the *Timaeus*, where he outlines his cosmology.
In contrast to the lofty considerations in the *Republic*
and the *Phaedo*, in his cosmology Plato speaks of
something at the very depths, what underlies the things

---

4   *Republic* 509c, F.M. Cornford trans., Oxford University Press, new York, 1968.

we see and deal with but is itself in no way an object.[5] It is what he calls the receptacle of all becoming, the place or space of things seen while it remains unseen. It is indeterminate, unknowable in any strict sense, not an object to a subject. He says that "we shall not be deceived if we call it a nature invisible and characterless, all-receiving, partaking in some very puzzling way of the intelligible and very hard to apprehend."[6]

In what he calls a likely story Plato speaks of the divine craftsman who brings about our world. He looks to the intelligible ideas or forms above and imprints them on the ever-yielding receptacle below to bring about our world much as a baker with his cookie cutter gives form to the soft dough to make a cookie he had in mind. In this way Plato has three levels of existence. First, the eternal Form, then copies of these that come and go in space and time, what we think of as actual things, then, as he puts it, "Third is Space which is everlasting, not admitting destruction; providing a situation for all things that come into being, but itself apprehended without the senses by a sort of bastard reasoning, hardly an object of belief."[7] With the timeless forms of intelligibility glistening high above we are to see down below what in itself is devoid of form but what can take on form, a receptive emptiness. Many have commented on the similarity of this Platonic indeterminateness to some Eastern notions of emptiness.

We can now see that notions at the upper, the middle, and the lower limits of Plato's philosophy

---

5   *Timaeus* 51a, Plato's *Cosmology*, F. M. Cornford, Routledge & Kegan Paul Limited, London,1948

6   ibid.

7   ibid. 52a-b

there is puzzling obscurity. At the top there is the idea of good that is blinding and beyond being, in the middle there is the soul that is in its true nature non-individual, and beneath the transient things there is the indeterminate receptacle apprehended only by a bastard knowing. These obscurities do seem to invite a Buddhist interpretation, and indeed His Holiness found them much more congenial than many Plato scholars do.

So can virtue be taught? I had asked His Holiness to draw on his own tradition to see how he would respond to that question, and it was clear he had thought about it carefully. Our discussion rounded things off this way. The true mind and its virtue cannot be taught, for, as the Buddha and Socrates would agree, it is there all along. Although typically we turn away from our true mind into the distractions of this world, we can come to it again. We then need to "recollect" the true self by much meditative discipline and practice. As with Socrates we only regain what is there all along.

Even if there is this important similarity, the difference between East and West comes out here again, as we have seen. For Socrates/Plato what we re-cognize is the intelligibility we can come to as we understand objectively and go beyond a personal perspective; while in Buddhism we dissolve into the Buddha-mind that is impersonal and non-conceptual openness. In purely conceptual understanding as well as in Buddhism there is a final lucidity, and in both any notion of "you" and "I" is dissolved. Virtue is accordingly the developed capacity to attain such illumination.

Then again, Can virtue be taught? Meno did not understand Socrates' response to his question, and surely he would not appreciate the Buddha's response either. But in either case, I think we can see what Meno would not: to teach is to lead up from distraction and obscurity to the light of our true minds. I think both Socrates and the Buddha could accept this conclusion while regarding final clarity and the activity leading to it in quite different ways.

I asked his Holiness if he would address another issue, this one regarding the teacher. I had read that one who holds steadfast to the path to enlightenment, a bodhisattva, having come right to the edge of nirvana, steps back in order to lead the life of the teacher showing others the way out of suffering and bondage. He stops short of his own full happiness in nirvana and remains in this world as compassionate teacher. This was said to be true of the Buddha. His Holiness said he was not so sure. Having reached enlightenment and nirvana one can return to this world as anything at all, and certainly the Buddha is the primary example of the enlightened one. I made a note to pursue this further another time to see why one having achieved enlightenment not only could but would return as the teacher. There is a parallel in Plato's depiction of the philosopher who, seeing the light of the idea of good, somehow also sees that he must leave the high and free activity of dialectic and return to the darkness of the Cave and try to bring others into the light.

Before leaving the Greeks I told the monks of an early meeting of Greeks and Indians. They had not heard of Socrates or Plato before the class, but they had heard of Alexander the Great. I told them he took a philosopher named Pyrrho with him as he conquered his way to India.

As the reports say, Pyrrho associated with the naked philosophers in India. What he learned from them was their technique of being able to show that no matter what anyone claims the opposite is just as likely. This allowed one to suspend judgment; and thereby being free from controversy, one is able to reach and maintain tranquility. He took this technique back to Greece, and he and his followers became known as Skeptics. It is not clear that they brought much tranquility in those uncertain early Hellenistic times, but skepticism as a mode of thought, a way to doubt whatever is claimed, lasted through the centuries.

Almost two thousand years after Pyrrho, a Frenchman, René Descartes, turned doubt in quite a different direction, one that would have astonished Pyrrho. Descartes devised a procedure he called methodical doubt to reach, not suspension of judgment and tranquility, but certainty of judgment. Certainty? Yes, and from that certainty there followed the opportunity to understand ourselves, the existence of God, and the whole natural world before us. What would Pyrrho say to that? What would a Buddhist say to that?

chapter 2
I think therefore I am?

Cogito, ergo sum. Let us follow convention and speak of this famous proposition simply as the *cogito* that shows the certainty of my existence, because I think. What will my thoughtful Buddhist monks make of it?

René Descartes found the crystalline clarity and certainty that mathematics can offer woefully lacking in the philosophy, theology, and science he had studied. Finding all that he had been taught uncertain, he saw a way to exploit such uncertainty. He set out quite deliberately to doubt everything he had been taught and even common sense (Am I really sitting in this room? It could be a dream.) in order to find some one thing that he could not doubt. As is well known, he found that no matter how far-reaching his doubt was, one thing was indubitable: that he doubted. One thing was certain, that he was there thinking. *Cogito ergo sum.*

When Pyrrho said no claim is any more true than

its opposite, it did not take long for a clever follower to ask him if he does not take that claim to be more true than its opposite. Pyrrho replied, "Not even that one," and went on his tranquil way. Descartes went further but then stopped. He could doubt the world out there, that two plus three make five, that God exists, indeed he could doubt everything. But *that he doubted* he could not doubt, without, of course, doubting. He had something certain, and doubting is brought to a halt in a certainty.

Early on, thinking about what I would try to convey of Western philosophy, I wondered what a Buddhist would make of the *cogito*, and I fully expected to be surprised. Certainly the move Descartes makes right after the *cogito* from thinking to an eternal soul doing the thinking would be most suspect. After showing the certainty of thought in the *cogito*, Descartes goes further, "I now admit nothing that is not necessarily true: I am therefore, precisely speaking, only a thinking thing, that is, a mind (*mens sive animus*), understanding, or reason—terms whose significance was before unknown to me. I am, however, a real thing, and really existent; but what thing? The answer was, a thinking thing."[8]

In contrast, a Buddhist could agree to there being thought (and relative knowledge), but the existence decided thereby is a distraction from true, impersonal mind. The ego is an illusion.

---

8   Rene Descartes, *Meditations*, John Veitch trans., The Rationalists, Anchor Books, Doubleday & Company, Garden City, New York, 1974.

Kalimpong. Photo by the author.

The monks took longer than I expected to sense the bite of the *cogito*, the sharp logic, the self-referential absurdity of doubting that one doubts, the craziness of thinking that one is not thinking. But when, once again, I resorted to *sherab* and *yeshe* they could get into the implications if still not the tight logic. With just a bit of prodding they saw that in focusing on the self as ego, a "thinking thing" as Descartes says, one is thinking at the level of conceptual thinking, *sherab*. We can focus clearly on an object, our own ego, but such clear but limited thought falls short of *yeshe*, non-conceptual true mind. The ego is an illusion as are all individual things, and the more one focuses on things the further one is from true, timeless, non-individual mind. In thinking then on his individual ego, Descartes does not exist as true mind: *cogito, ergo non sum*. I rather expected the monks would come to this.

Can it go the other way also? If I think at the level of *yeshe*, or rather, allow "I think" to mean the ultimate realization of true mind of itself, then it follows that I do not exist as an individual ego. Again from the opposite direction, *cogito ergo non sum*. Some of the monks expressed a reluctance to see *yeshe* as a mode of thought at all, and surely they are right about that if thought involves a subject attending an object. But even so it can be claimed that at that level of true mind beyond subjects and objects, the individual ego does not exist.

From the very first, Descartes' thought stimulated much criticism; indeed, even to the present day, some philosophers take pains to offer a critique of Descartes to show how they avoid the problems he left us. One that we have already seen and will address later is Descartes' move from thinking to a thinker, from ongoing thought to a persisting thinking thing, as he calls the mind, a substance that has thinking as its essential attribute. This notion of a substance with an essential attribute, which for all his methodical doubt he took over un-challenged from Aristotelian/Thomistic theology of his day, many soon claimed is not established in the *cogito*. Thinking, yes; a thinker, well, it can be doubted. The complementary body/mind dualism, the problem of free will in a mechanical physical world, the denigration of the senses, and many other problems are still targets of critique. But the monks' mode of critique I had not run across. If that is what it is.

Is our treatment of the *cogito*, aside from being a bit facile, a legitimate criticism at all? Formally the claim could be: *If* there is a true mind beyond individual mind showing the individual mind to be an illusion, then the individual mind does not truly exist. But how can the *If* of the initial proposition be removed? Can any amount of argument establish what is claimed as the true mind? If not, then the conclusion, *cogito ergo non sum*, remains hypothetical and falls way short of the certainty of Descartes' *cogito ergo sum*. But then this is just the sort of thought that *yeshe* takes us beyond; argument is empty. The only way to attain a non-conceptual, indeed thought-less, doubt-less finality is by lengthy discipline, vigorous dialectic that removes itself as it self-destructs, and lengthy meditation.

His Holiness the 17th Karmapa Trinley Thaye Dorje studying with the author. Photo by Jachi Shiu.

In our private session His Holiness moved quickly to this point as I pressed toward the sense of finality in Buddhism that is distinct from Descartes' logical certainty. We moved to the openness disclosed in *yeshe* in which there cannot be any doubt because there are no explicit thoughts at all. Doubt is obliterated. If all doubt dissolves, is certainty the result? But then if *yeshe* is devoid of all thought, wouldn't certainty be obliterated also? At the level of *yeshe*, or enlightened mind, we are beyond doubt and beyond certainty. Certainty is within what we have been calling intellectual clarity, to hold in contrast with the enlightenment of *yeshe*, and hence *yeshe* can obliterate doubt, but cannot then usher us into intellectual certainty.

Yet there is something like certainty in enlightenment, something final and unmovable. We are on the major divide in our major theme, enlightenment versus intellectual certainty. Those who have reached enlightenment can claim a finality in ultimate wisdom, but they cannot then move to intellectual certainty. The others, including Descartes, who have not reached such finality and have quite another sense of certainty in mind, may have certainty but are left with no avenue to enlightened finality. Can enlightened finality supercede certainty as *yeshe* supercedes *sherab*? From the other side, can intellectual certainty recognize enlightened finality? In our last chapter we will face some of the problems foreshadowed here.

There are other ways to bridge a divide. As we gave the *cogito* a few turns, it became somewhat playful and humorous as it so often did in classes at home, and the monks were smiling and quietly laughing. There have been so many jokes and humorous changes rung on the *cogito* I need not add any here, but also those devoted to meditative practice have been the butt of many jokes also. I recall a cartoon in the *New Yorker* that shows two shaven-headed young men sitting in meditation, and one says out of the side of his mouth to the other, "Are you not thinking what I am not thinking?" This is humorous but also thereby significant. Theorists say one essential condition of humor is a sudden shift of context; we are thinking along one line of thought in one context and suddenly we are triggered to think along another line of thought in another context and see that the second together with the first is an absurd conjunction, This along with other conditions can bring us to laugh. It is that conjunction that interests me, for it shows that in order to see humor in a conjunction both contexts have to be held in mind. I conclude that only if the monks can understand the Cartesian position to some degree can they then see it humorously conjoined to a Buddhist context, and the more they entertain that contrast of the two the keener the insight into both can become.

I hope this point can also hold, minus the humor perhaps, for our major theme, so that we can see both *enlightenment* and *intellectual clarity* more clearly in their contrast with one another. That was certainly the case in my discussions with His Holiness. But the question remains: from what viewpoint can we see the contrast?

Needless to say, Descartes' next major step, arguments to prove the existence of God, did not impress the monks. They thought the arguments and their purpose were at best curiosities. Because God or a god is not an issue in Buddhism, Descartes' efforts seemed pointless to them. Descartes' causal argument (I have the idea of a perfect being, but being imperfect I could not be the cause of such an idea, hence there must be another cause sufficient to that effect, namely the perfect being, God) they found interesting since, so I thought, they were accustomed to thinking causally, and they could insert their own sense of perfect being. The other arguments did not impress them, neither their logical form nor their purpose.

In trying to make Descartes' arguments clear I was reminded how much of Western thought involves a final referent, some pinnacle atop the pyramid of understanding. There is Plato's idea of good, Aristotle's unmoved mover, God in theology, of course, and science is dedicated to some notion of enduring intelligibility or laws of nature, whether God's wisdom or not. Atheism, of course, takes its identity by opposing such an idea and is thus infected by it. This was made all the more vivid in my efforts to show the monks the critical position of God in Descartes' metaphysics while they are in a tradition devoid of such a referent. I think it would take much longer than my five weeks to lead the monks to see what is so typical in Western thought.

Descartes' *cogito* that establishes an individual mind as the basis of all inquiry encouraged the development of the individualism so characteristic of modern Western culture. The individual thinking substance is where we begin. A similar emphasis on the individual person is found a half a century after Descartes in England in the works of John Locke. Though at pains to stand off from Descartes' rationalism, Locke put forth in his opposing empirical approach an individual mind just as pivotal. All knowledge comes from experience, and that consists in perceptions and reflections, imprinting themselves on the mind that is initially a blank tablet, a *tabula rasa*. Being essentially blank, each mind is equal to every other, or as we know it, all men are created free and equal. Locke elaborated that idea in his political philosophy, and subsequent history takes it to our Constitution and beyond. There is individualism prominent in both the rationalist and empiricist philosophy that complemented the focus on the individual in politics, economics, and religion in the 18th and 19th centuries in the West.

Needless to say, this individualism is curious and even disturbing from a Buddhist point of view. As mentioned early on, the Karmapa found the Socratic concept of virtue selfish, and here this modern individualism is deliberately even more selfish. Such emphasis distracts us from the non-individual, non-conceptual Buddha mind. A Buddhist would find it curious that Locke regards individuals as so many separate blank tablets rather than as really blank and hence devoid of individuality and hence one pervasive emptiness. We will see in Chapter Four if empiricism can take that blankness seriously.

I left it at that because I wanted to press on to the *Sixth Meditation* where Descartes comes to the physical world and our knowledge of it via mathematical physics. I knew from talking with some of the monks outside class that they had a genuine curiosity about modern science, and I hoped to exploit that.

chapter 3
Is science a distraction?

Friedrich Nietzsche was one of Socrates' most appreciative and at the same time most severe critics. Toward the end of his career he added to his earliest work, *The Birth of Tragedy*, what he called an "Attempt at Self Criticism." In a brilliant second paragraph he turns to the theoretical man—the man of philosophy, science, mathematics—and asks a most intriguing question: "And science itself, our science— indeed what is the significance of all science, viewed as a symptom of life?" He goes on:

> For what—worse, *whence*—all science? How now? Is the resolve to be so scientific about everything perhaps a kind of fear of, an escape from, pessimism? A subtle last resort against—*truth*? And, morally speaking, a sort of cowardice and falseness?

Amorally speaking, a ruse? O Socrates, Socrates, was that perhaps *your* secret? O enigmatic ironist, was that perhaps your—irony?[9]

We usually see Socratic irony as he claims to be ignorant of the truth and entices his interlocutor to join him in the quest for it. Here Nietzsche sees that whole enterprise—philosophy, science, all disciplined inquiry—as a dodge, a bulwark against the truth. And Socrates knew it, hence the deeper irony of his irony.

And the truth? In the *Birth of Tragedy* Nietzsche tells the story of King Midas, famous for his golden touch. He catches Silenus, the king of the satyrs, and asks him what is the best for man, and the satyr, after some prodding, replies, "What is best of all is utterly beyond your reach: not to be born, not to *be*, to be *nothing*. But the second best for you is—to die soon."[10]2 These are odd words coming from the king of the raunchy, frolicking satyrs. We are to see from this story that we are thrown into life only to face terror, pain, and death; to the wise, oblivion is preferable. In flight from that dark truth we could follow the Dionysian satyrs into orgiastic drunken stupefaction, or from that same dark truth we could take flight into what Nietzsche calls Apollonian illusion and the dream world of art or the vision of a new clarity promised by science. In either case, we distract ourselves from the dark and terrifying truth of our existence.

---

9   *The Birth of Tragedy*, Walter Kaufmann trans., Vintage Books, New York, 1967, p.18.

10   ibid. p. 42. Kaufmann refers to Sophocles, Oedipus at Colonus, lines 1224ff.

The Karma Shri Diwakar Institute of Buddhist Studies. Photo by the author.

I put these odd reflections on science at the beginning of our discussion to let the disciplined inquiry most obvious in the natural sciences be not only something to admire but something to question. Typically, in our Western schooling we are taught to try to see things objectively, and the scope and successes of this point of view cannot be sufficiently admired. But from what perspective may objectivity and science itself be seen? Let that question hang over our closer look at science.

Descartes offered one such perspective, indeed one that nurtured incipient modern science. He is rightly regarded as the father of modern philosophy, for he not only made a deliberate break from medieval philosophy and theology by his methodical doubt, but he also offered a new world-view within which we see a place for science and the form it must take.

Having established the mind with certainty, and thence a benevolent God, Descartes can then return to what he originally suspended by doubt, a real God-guaranteed external physical world. We can have clear mathematical conceptions of this world. Then, because we naturally believe there are physical things out there, and because we are certain God is not a deceiver, we can be certain a real physical nature lies before us and can be known by reason in clear and distinct concepts.

Descartes offers a simple example. With our five senses we may perceive a cube of wax and see its color, and with traces of honey still there we can note its smell and taste, and if we tap it we can hear a sound and feel its solidity. When we put it near the fire, however, all such sense qualities disappear; it is a transparent puddle with no color, no smell, no taste, and no longer a solid we can feel or tap to make a sound. All sense qualities have changed, and yet we regard it as the same wax. How so? What remains the same when the sensed qualities change?

It is material substance that lies beneath the outer qualities. The qualities can come and go, but the underlying matter itself remains the same, and this is not apprehended by the senses but by reason in clear concepts. It was the same matter that was solid and then liquid. And what is matter essentially? As we learned in school, matter is what can take up space, or as Descartes would prefer, extension is the essential attribute of matter. It is essentially extended in various modes, e.g., shape and size that can be made clear in solid geometry. As mind has thought as its essential attribute, so material substance has the essential attribute of extension, Matter can be perceived by the senses with secondary qualities like color and smoothness, but these exist only in our perception, and they come and go. It is reason that conceives the essential nature of matter in mathematical lucidity. So what is the wax? It is material substance with primary *quantitative* attributes; its perceivable qualities are secondary. They depend on an observer, and can change while the material substance remains the same.

To a Buddhist, of course, the sensed qualities of an object are an illusion, but so too is the allegedly real and extended material substance underlying the sensed qualities. Both parts of Descartes' dualism, mental substance certain of itself and material substance known in the clear and distinct ideas of mathematics, are illusions. This mind/matter dualism makes explicit precisely what we move beyond in ultimate wisdom where there is no subject and no object.

We saw that Descartes himself, by his methodical doubt, moved beyond the prevailing wisdom of his day. After the monumental theology of St. Thomas Aquinas that incorporated much of Aristotelian philosophy, what was regarded as science was to the pattern elaborated by Aristotle. The Pythagorean and Platonic confidence that the world is structured mathematically had given way in some four hundred years before Descartes to the Aristotelian confidence that it is structured logically, i.e., in accordance with Aristotelian logic of subjects with their qualities as predicates. Here is the familiar example. All earthly living things are mortal, all men are living things and hence are mortal, In the familiar expression: All men are mortal; Socrates is a man; therefore, Socrates is mortal. Such logic was the form and language of science in the medieval period. Mathematics was to be regarded as a separate science, not the language of all the sciences. But Galileo showed quite dramatically that such a science fails in the face of carefully detected, that is, measured, that is, quantified empirical evidence. This testing of a theory against empirical evidence is what we need to see more clearly as the beginning of modern science.

If it is the case, as the science of the day had it, that a heavy object in seeking its natural place downward falls faster than a lighter object of the same size, then clearly if two such objects are dropped simultaneously from a tower, the heavier object will hit the ground before the lighter object. More formally, if a theory is correct, then certain evidence will be observed. If the evidence is not forthcoming, the theory is false. The story is that Galileo performed the experiment from the Leaning Tower of Pisa, and the light and heavy objects hit the ground at the same time. Therefore, the theory is false. Actually, Galileo rolled balls down an inclined plane in a much more carefully controlled and measurable experiment to show that light and heavy balls roll down the inclined plane covering the same distance in the same time, but the story of the Tower could also be true and is more dramatic. In any case, we see part of how the scientific method works; by careful experiment it can disprove a theory.

Can it prove a theory? If the theory is true, certain evidence will be forthcoming. Sure enough the evidence appears. Therefore, what? We want to say that the theory is then proved, but of course that does not follow. For example, if it rains, the ground will be wet. The ground is wet. It may have rained, but it could be wet for some other reason. Further experience could bring its rejection, and a new theory proposed. And tested.

Kalimpong. Photo by the author.

I wanted to stress this bit of the logic of scientific method, its lack of finality in verifying a theory and its ongoing and progressive nature, to show how research has become so important in the modern world. Later in our course when we make the nature of time our topic this progressive nature of science will be an important consideration.

The monks, as far as I could tell, had little trouble with the logic of scientific method, but it was clear their curiosity about science had not been satisfied. They wanted to hear more about the big bang and black holes. But before I tried my hand at conveying something about those fascinating concepts, I wanted to show them something of the shift from Newtonian physics to relativity and quantum theory. They could follow, I think, my layman's sketch of that shift, but they were still more interested in particular results than the theories themselves. I doubt that my eventual popular science treatment of the big bang and black holes was all that satisfying either, but I could see how those considerations and the monks' reaction might also be helpful when we consider the nature of time.

At our next meeting His Holiness was ready to discuss the darker issues mentioned at the start of this chapter. He was quite well informed about science and expressed his fascination with it. He found the theory of the big bang intensely interesting and disturbing, as a Buddhist should, if it means absolutely everything had a beginning. Similarly, concepts of black holes were fascinating and puzzling. Can something be sucked into a black hole never to escape, never to be reborn, never be a part of the cycle of time? But then this fascination was itself the problem for the Karmapa. The more we become enthralled with natural and ordinary things, which means, the more we are taken by illusion, the more we are distracted from Buddhism's ultimate truth which goes beyond things and concepts.

There are any number of ways to be bound or distracted from the path to enlightenment; we can lead a life devoted to gaining pleasure, wealth, fame, or power, none of which is all that admirable. But we can also be devoted to gaining knowledge, that is, relative knowledge, of natural things—the hard sciences, but also historical events and archeological finds, psychological and sociological phenomena, or whatever can arrest the inquiring mind. His Holiness spoke of all such knowledge as relative knowledge to be seen in contrast with ultimate truth. Relative knowledge, being of things impermanent, falls short of ultimate and timeless truth that is gained only after lengthy meditative practice. What is achieved is a timeless final truth devoid of objects and devoid of subjects. Nothing is permanent. Buddhists can enjoy the ambiguity of that statement.

Granted, science is one of the better distractions, but being all the more enthralling it is also all the more binding to what is impermanent and illusory.

His Holiness surprised me when he spoke of the major distractions in the realm of desire: first food, second clothes, and third fame. Fame? Yes, for all of these desires need to be seen in a wider scope. He did not say it, but I took food to stand for all bodily desires, and I thought clothing was simple enough, to protect us from thorns and the cold. But no, by clothes he meant how we announce ourselves, our station, our role, and in general how we think people should regard us. And it is by our clothes that they do judge us. This leads right into the third, fame, the regard others have for us.

I remarked that fame is something he is destined to have to deal with more and more and that he already deals with it admirably. I went on to say I had never detected the slightest hint of arrogance in him. After a pause he said, "Perhaps not now, but later with big events, who knows?" He agreed it is like bravery. You may be confident you can face the enemy, but you don't really know until you march into battle. I have every confidence in him.

The giant of modern philosophy, Immanuel Kant, also held that science is only knowledge of appearance and not of the real thing in itself, and he saw no way for the real thing in itself to be reached. All we have is experience, i.e., appearance, and a recognition that it falls short of knowledge of the real thing in itself. But within experience, i.e. within our empirical world that we take to be real, we can have scientific knowledge, i.e., knowledge of how things really do appear to us.

We face, then, the notable Kantian question: How is science possible? We start with perceptions that come and go, and they are always from an individual, i.e., subjective viewpoint, and yet we can make judgments about experience that can claim to be objective and hold universally. We do have science, but how is it possible?

For example, anyone looking down railroad tracks sees the tracks converge, even to a point if the terrain is flat, yet no sane person will claim that the tracks actually converge. If all those looking see the convergence, how can all confidently judge the tracks actually do not converge but remain parallel? How is that judgment possible? Given our individual subjective perceptions, how is an objective judgment possible, i.e., how is science possible?

In class I gave a sketch of what Kant would call a deduction to show that for any experience of an object, a formal unity of the subject, a unity of apperception, is presupposed as a necessary condition. We can see an object as a persisting unity only if a single observer brings together the variety of data perceived as a single thing. For example, we may observe the front of a house, then a side, then the back and other side in a sequence, but in our judgment we do not claim the house exists in a sequence, this side and then that side; no, we take all these data together as a single, persisting thing, the house. In a characteristic statement that at first jolts the understanding but on subsequent thought can be recognized as putting the matter as clearly as possible, Kant says that "an *object* is that in the concept of which the manifold of a given intuition is *united*."[11] The necessary condition of our achieving this unity is the formal unity of any observer's apprehension. In short, an experience of any object as a unity presupposes the unity of apperception. After a few more examples—the sun and the moon appear to be almost the same size, yet combined with other data—I believe the monks caught the drift.

Interestingly, the monks could appreciate Kant's conception of an object more readily than they could Descartes' conception. Descartes' example of the piece of wax to show how reason apprehends material substance underlying outer appearance did not impress them, but the Kantian example of the house being a synthesis we make of an array of data did make sense to them.

After the class, His Holiness expressed favorable regard of Kant's deduction. Both he and Kant would agree we are dealing only with appearance and not with reality, but granting that, Kant shows how science is nevertheless possible within appearance. He shows how relative knowledge, as His Holiness would speak of knowledge within experience, can become as impressive as it is in scientific achievements. I surmised it was that capacity, that possibility of making universally valid judgments about what we experience, that His Holiness had seen as a problem. If what we confront is illusion, how can there be science? Kant's contribution fills the need; the subject provides the formal unity that is the condition of any experience of any object, and because that formal unity holds universally, scientific judgments, or universally valid judgments of matters of fact, are

---

11 Immanuel Kant, *Critique of Pure Reason*, B137, Norman Kemp Smith trans. The Modern Library, New York, 1958

possible. In bringing perceptions together as objects, we construct our world.

That the mind constructs our world is compatible with the Buddhist position, and so too is Kant's claim that the empirical ego, what we detect as we reflect on ourselves, is also a construction, i.e., taking an array of data together as a single thing, the self. To paraphrase Kant's statement above, the self is that in the concept of which a given stream of consciousness is united. The Karmapa found this much more acceptable than Descartes' *cogito* that was intended to show with certainty a mental substance underlying our thought.

It sounds odd, but science has a place within illusion as do the empirical egos of the scientists and the rest of us. The world and the self are both our constructions.

His Holiness agreed that science is the best way to come to know, that is, to have relative knowledge, of the world, and he is a great admirer of science for that reason. We do face and have to deal with actual things, impermanent as they are, and science illuminates the impermanent world marvelously. I suppose that such knowledge is *sherab*, but beyond that is *yeshe*. And there is the rub. Being engrossed in the world means we are all the more distracted, all the more bound and in need of freedom, all the farther from *yeshe*.

We saw at the beginning that Nietzsche depicted science as a distraction, a dodge, a protection against the truth, but that truth is the wisdom of Silenus: to be born, to be individuated, is to face terror, pain, and death. It is from that truth that art and science would distract us. We lack the strength to face the truth of life's terror and resort to Apollonian illusions or Dionysian drunken oblivion of any sense of a self. The claim could be that a reveler thereby becomes one with the life force itself, Dionysus, but only briefly. Then what? If we soften the initial expressions just slightly and say that in being individuated we face a life of suffering, we can see, or be reminded of, a better way. That is where the Buddha begins. There is a way out of suffering and on to the freedom of enlightenment.

So is science a distraction? Kant would readily agree, indeed insist, it has its place only in appearance, but it would take more persuasion than we could muster to get him to say it is a distraction. Nietzsche would see it as a symptom of decline and a forced cheerfulness to cover over dark truth, and the Buddhist would see it as an enthralling distraction from the ultimate truth. And the good scientist himself? He might want to see an occasion for further research. But how?

The perspective Descartes offers within which we can view science has given way, or is giving way, and this points up the question again: From what perspective can the meaning of science be viewed? The question itself is liberating and could make a Buddhist smile.

chapter 4
How far can empiricism go?

We read *Hamlet* or see it enacted on stage, and at the end we close the book or see the curtain come down. It will be read or enacted again. Of course, Hamlet in the play and any number of other vivid fictional characters are endlessly interesting; indeed, as with Hamlet, we can understand more about his character every time we open the book and read or see the curtain go up and watch. But what are these personages? We certainly do not look for a soul substance that survives every reading and every enactment, some invisible entity that flits from one reading or performance to another. No, we attend the play again and recognize the same character in the narrative, indeed, as narrative, as the cluster of thoughts, words, expressions, and actions connected in a pattern to make up a personality. Now here is our question: How are actual people different? Is the self a narrative, a cluster and pattern of thoughts, actions and experiences? On another occasion in *As You Like It*, Jacques, a colorful philosopher, says,

> All the world's a stage,
> And all the men and women merely players, They have their exits and their entrances, And one man in his time plays many parts, His acts being seven ages.

Kalimpong. Photo by the author.

This may seem an odd introduction to David Hume, but in our segment on empiricism I wanted to stress Hume's treatment of personal identity, thinking it would be congenial with the monks and be more interesting than lingering over his opposition to Cartesian rationalism and other meta-physical and anti-metaphysical issues. Many have remarked on similarities in Mahayana Buddhism and Hume's empiricism, especially on the issue of personal identity, and that is what I wanted to explore. One of the first questions outsiders ask Buddhists is focused on reincarnation, and once they learn of the Buddha's rejection of the Hindu notion of an individual soul that survives the death of one body to be reborn in another, they have to wonder just what is it that is reborn.

Jachi Shiu joined us to make photographs of the school, our classes, and my conferences with the Karmapa. When she asked him if he minded her doing that he replied, "Not at all. I am used to it." I am sure he is, and he remained just as much at ease as ever.

Hume's empiricism is very simple, but with extensive implications. All knowledge comes from experience, but more explicitly that means we start with perceptions given by the senses and feelings, and from these, and only from these, we derive ideas. There are no innate ideas as the rationalists claim, but rather any idea can be reduced to the originating perception or perceptions. If, then, we have the idea of a soul, we must show the perception or perceptions from which it is derived. Already, clearly it is futile to claim the soul is something underlying our experiences while it is itself not perceivable. All one can come to are other perceptions or ideas; even the idea that there is something underlying experience is itself just another idea. To claim evidence of something beyond experience keeps you within experience and shows that the claim is absurd. As Hume has it, "When I turn my reflexion on *myself*, I can never perceive this *self* without some one or more perceptions. 'Tis the composition of these, therefore, which forms the self."[12]

---

12 *A Treatise of Human Nature*, Appendix, p. 634, L. A. Selby-Bigge ed., Oxford at the Clarendon Press, 1965.

Descartes can claim without doubt that there is thinking, but an empiricist can point out that to go on and say there is a substantial thinker having the thought is just to express more thought, more ideas.

Hume had difficulties with his own position on personal identity, for the notion of a composition of perceptions in an object or a scene and of a causal sequence of perceptions required a recognition of *relations* among the perceptions. But because, as he has it, each perception is a distinct existent with no essential relation to another, then the relation itself is elusive. To have evidence of it would require yet another perception, and then its relation is the problem, and so forth. The relation is as far from direct evidence as a soul entity is. Hume concludes, "Did our perceptions either inhere in something simple and individual, or did the mind perceive some real connexion among them, there would be no difficulty in the case. For my part, I must plead the privilege of a sceptic, and confess, that this difficulty is too hard for my understanding."[13]

There are purposes beyond epistemological niceties. Descartes says his philosophy supports Christian theology, for he has rational proof that the soul exists, is separate from the body, and hence can survive death. A personal identity is essential in this idea. Aside from theological concerns, the empirical position has a problem also, as we saw. In Hume's view, just what is it that allows a person to regard himself or herself as an individual who endures and changes through time? The changing sequence of experiences is given, but what is it that endures or repeats? What is it that allows one to

13   ibid. p. 634

say, "I am the same person I was yesterday and indeed was years before, and perhaps will be after my death?" All the experiences are different, but what is the same?

The issue here between Descartes and Hume rehearses one that drew much thought and controversy in India centuries, indeed millennia before, ever since the Buddha himself rejected the notion, prevalent in his day and in ours, that each of us has an individual soul. I was surprised then in class that one of the monks assumed without further ado that he had an individual soul that would survive him and be reborn. His peers gently dissented, but the Karmapa just watched and remained silent.

He told me why in our discussion after class. He said both claims, that there is an enduring individual soul and the claim that there is only a cluster of experiences, could at best be only relative knowledge. Each had appeals. To think of one's self as a single enduring soul helps explain much experience, e.g., how I am the same person today I was yesterday, and makes the notion of rebirth seem understandable. The other claim is more thoughtful and shows more easily how one can move beyond the welter of experiences that make up the self to the serenity of the non-individual Buddha mind, for the notion of an individual soul with its cravings and disappointments is among the fetters entangling us in *samsara*. Because the Buddha explicitly rejects the first, I asked His Holiness to say more about the second.

He suggested we think of the self of this world as a stream of mind (I immediately thought of William James' idea of the stream of consciousness); and because such a self is shaped by causal factors in a single life, such causes (*karma*) can continue and have effects beyond one lifetime and shape what we would call another self. It is the causal continuity that allows us to see our self as enduring from day to day, year to year; and the causal pattern can continue beyond an individual life. Unfortunately, just as we came to this major Buddhist theme our time was up, and the Karmapa had other obligations.

My own thought moved on to the notion of the self as narrative expressed at the beginning of this chapter. A careful reader of a literary work can detect the causes that shape a character, and sure enough those causes are at work in the next reading, and the character is the same. I hope this notion of a person as a narrative at least suggests the right path. Compatible with this is Hume's remark, "The mind is a kind of theatre, where several perceptions successively make their appearance; pass, re-pass, glide away, and mingle in an infinite variety of postures and situations."[14]

So how far can empiricism go? It cannot probe beneath experience to detect a soul substance that Hindus and Cartesians speak of, nor can empiricism ascend above experience to an enduring unity and ultimate truth beyond doubt and skepticism. Hume is content with his skeptical middle position.

There is another way to test the limits of empiricism. Hume's claim that each perception is a distinct existent can be put to the test. Is that what we actually see, is it empirically founded? If Hume were a more attentive empiricist, he would see that within the oval of our visual field, in which anything visible has its place, only the smallest part is clear and seen as a distinct existent. It is

---

14   ibid. p. 253

only in the center of our visual field where we focus, say on the corner of a book nearby, that we see anything as distinct, and even a fraction of an inch around it, say the title on the cover, the shapes and colors are indistinct, the tile unreadable. Or here now focus steadily on any word, no, on any letter, in this sentence and notice that letters and words next in the line or in the line above or below are blurred, unreadable unless we shift our focus. Further from the center, there is a general blurring toward a surrounding indeterminacy that is always there. That is what vision displays, but we are typically so concerned only with what we focus on in the center that we disregard the vastly greater surrounding indistinct display and around that and beyond our peripheral vision the completely indeterminate from which all our perceptions emerge. We rarely notice the surrounding empty void; indeed, to notice almost always means to give our attention to the center of our visual field where perceptions can be clear. It is that distinct center that Hume takes as the sole example of the empirically given, distinct perceptions that are separate and devoid of relations. Then, he has the problem of finding relations in this array of perceptions otherwise as chaotic as a spray of confetti. But visual perceptions are not sharp-edged distinct existences; they are blurred and more or less indistinct, and they are in a continuum. In short, Hume was not a sufficiently sensitive empiricist. Let us start with a more sensitive empiricism and see how far we can go. Further, let us consider only the visual.

This is the experiment I tried with the monks seated in front of me. Sit quietly and focus on some point, again the corner of a book will do, and do not shift the eyes to see something else more clearly. Still focused on the corner notice, as just mentioned, that even a fraction of an inch around that point things are indistinct and blurred, not in focus. To focus on a point, as a psychologist can show us, the eyes are quite busy dancing around the point, and of course they are slightly triangulated toward the point. Hold that for awhile, but then calmly let your eyes stop dancing around the point and relax the triangulation as though looking at the horizon. It may take awhile. Now everything, including what was clear in the center, is now blurry and indistinct.

I am taking a lead from my old teacher, F. S. C. Northrop here,[15] and he speaks of this now blurry and indistinct oval field of vision as a differentiated aesthetic continuum, aesthetic in its literal meaning of perceptual. This first phase can come fairly easily; in fact many a student in class seems to reach it quite frequently as does a reader when things get too philosophical.

Exploit it now. Nothing is in clear focus; what we confront is a continuum of blurry shapes and colors, and toward the outer limits of the oval of vision, colors are reduced to barely distinguishable light or dark and shapes dissolve almost entirely. The next phase takes more patience, and I will have to consider only what we can barely anticipate as perceptual possibilities and rely on descriptions of others. What comes at this phase is a dissolving of all shapes and colors into an undifferentiated continuum, typically into a homogeneous beige as in the empty portion of a Chinese landscape painting.

The next possibility takes considerably more patience to come to, and here and now we can only speculate. The oval beige continuum is itself still differentiated from the surrounding totally colorless and shapeless

---

15 *The Meeting of East and West*, The Macmillan Company, New York, 1946

indeterminacy, and, moreover, it is still attended by the perceiver as differentiated from the continuum perceived. The subject-object relation still holds. Both of these differentiations can with considerably more patience gradually dissolve. The continuum is not even beige, and it is no longer perceived by an observer. The subject becomes indistinguishable from the undifferentiated continuum. *Shunyata*?

Kalimpong. Photo by the author.

So from Western empiricism taken to such a limit do we merge with Eastern enlightenment? Perhaps as a suggestive first step. In our progression we had to resort to speculation on possibilities, and though the phases could be traced as possibilities, the actual attainment takes much discipline and a long, long time; and, of course, it involves more than the visual. Where we had to lapse into speculation is near where Buddhists begin, for the obstacles lie within the self and its turmoil of thoughts and feelings. To say the subject can dissolve into the indeterminate is easy, but to attain such freedom and become the non-individual Buddha mind is, I dare say, rare indeed.

The monks were attentive and appreciative, but not impressed. I rather think their seeing this Westerner trying to deal with Eastern thought was on a par with my regard of them as they tried to deal with a problem in geometry. I ventured to suggest that the monks' curriculum include more mathematics, and they could just as well suggest that Western curricula include more of what I have just spoken of as a more sensitive empiricism.

To complement the quietude of enlightenment, there is another kind of empiricism in the monastery, a notably noisy one. Every afternoon before dinner the monks gather in the beautiful shrine for a service or *puja* called the Mahakala. There they sit in four rows, two on each side of the central Buddha figure, and the monks chant rhythmically reading from a traditional text in tribute to the wrathful deity Mahakala, and the repetitive melodic sound is soothing and, well, enchanting. Then, at appropriate times, I assumed at the end of a section, two monks vigorously beat on two colorful hanging drums each about four feet across. Then, two other monks sound two long ornate horns that reach to the floor. The drum beats are of such intensity and low frequency that you feel them in the viscera as much as hear them in the ears, and the whole body responds inwardly and memorably. The horns respond with low brackish notes that come with stridently sharp high frequency overtones, sonic lightning to the thunder of the drums. Resonating in the belly and the head, the sound can obliterate any lingering egoistic thoughts, and it melds one into a harmony, no, a unity with all beings near and far as the sound fills the room, the air around the *shedra*, and on to the distant mountains.

Most religious services appeal in some way to all the senses or most of them, and by repetition and sensuous impact they open one to deeper recognitions. The Mahakala puja is as impressive and memorable a service as I have ever experienced, even though I could not understand the Tibetan text. Empiricism as vivid experience can go very far, indeed. Its pedagogical impact is impressive but hard to specify. Both cerebral and visceral, the ancient ritual affects the whole person and, so I imagined, nurtures the integrity of the monks and their congeniality.

I can speak of the curriculum the monks follow only as an outsider looking in. The school is for advanced students of Buddhism, and they take courses on the intricacies of the Buddhist teachings, and as far as I can tell those teachings are every bit as complicated and challenging as courses in Western philosophy in our colleges and universities. In addition, they practice meditation, and, as I have already mentioned, they engage in lively debates. As a result they are, to all appearances, genuinely happy; they are remarkably good-natured with easy smiles and laughter. Their curriculum shapes the whole person remarkably, and they are fraternal with one another with little of the tensions, jealousies, and competitiveness I am familiar with. They seem to enjoy their schooling and being with one another.

So how far can empiricism go? Perhaps with Hume, to an appreciation of a self not defined by an individual soul entity, but by a narrative of experiences. Taking a broad view of empiricism we, noticed that intense ritual experience in the Mahakala can remind us of a deeper self beyond a personal narrative of experiences. With meditative practice that deeper self is attainable, and if that attainment can still be spoken of as experience, indeed, the ultimate experience, empiricism can take us to a freedom beyond a subject–object relation and to a happiness beyond pleasures.

A minor pleasure may come in imagining skeptical David Hume meditating.

chapter 5
What time is it?

A sense of time is so fundamental in our reflections on ourselves and the world that we just take it for granted. That people in other cultures have senses of time different from our own we can accept intellectually but can hardly imagine what it is like. We are born, we grow up, we survive, perhaps thrive, we die; that sequence is unavoidable brute fact. After death perhaps there is a long afterlife elsewhere. How could it be otherwise? The more things change, the more this pattern is the same. or: We are reborn from previous lives, grow up, survive, perhaps thrive, die, and will be reborn to re-live the pattern again and again. The cycle is endless unless we gain freedom from this *samsara* in enlightenment. How could it be otherwise? The more things change, the more this pattern remains the same.

The linear sense of time that shapes Western culture and thought contrasts with the cyclical sense of time that shapes Eastern culture and thought, and this contrast has held for centuries. Then the more things change, the more this contrast remains the same. But is it in linear time or cyclical time? What time is it?

It has been remarked that until recently India has produced no notable historians, and yet from a historian's point of view India has had from very ancient times as rich, varied, and significant a history as any people or region on earth. But there is a dearth of chroniclers. Many observers say even today there is little sense of history in Indian culture, and it was that curious difference from the West that prompted Erik to urge me to make that a topic to explore.

I pared down Hegel's *Introduction to the Philosophy of History* to the bare bones, just enough to clarify his claim that because science has shown that there is a rational pattern in the vastness of nature it is only reasonable to expect that there is a rational pattern in the vast sweep of history. To his own satisfaction he found that pattern, and it is not only linear but progressive. History is a march of a thesis provoking its antithesis culminating in a synthesis that shows itself as a thesis that then provokes its antithesis and so on until the final synthesis of a perfectly ordered state. Marx carried over a similar pattern despite all his other differences from Hegel. From feudalism, history moves to capitalism, and from there finally to socialism. Whether these grand ideological scenarios showing history as a dialectical progress can be seen in the actual course of history after Hegel is certainly debatable, but in any case some notion of progress was and is prevalent in Western culture.

That is the topic I wanted to stress, our Western notion of progress. Hegel was not a success with the monks, but once the notion of progress was filled in with some of their own experiences it became less foreign. No less than young people in the West are they attentive to advances in technology—more and better cell phones, better cameras, better sound equipment, better cars, airplanes, etc. There is obvious progress in technology, the cultural consequences aside. Earlier I had stressed the advancements in science and how the scientific method is the very engine of scientific progress, and they understood that well enough. Do such developments in any way threaten the Buddhist's larger view of time?

No. One's acculturated sense of time is so inclusive that even descriptions of other senses of time have to take their place within the prevailing structure. In our case, when we hear that Buddhists have a cyclical sense of time, we cannot help but put that concept within our linear sense of time and its attendant historical standpoint, and from that point see it as an ancient and curious but still held view of time. That in no way conveys what it is like actually to live and think within cyclical time. Conversely, a Buddhist could look with puzzled amazement at our drive toward an envisioned future all the while keeping an anxious eye on the clock and the calendar. That much Buddhists can see and understand, but even so they would not know what it is like to live and think within such linear time with all its urgencies. We must keep up and not fall behind what is the latest thing in fashion, in the use of new technical gadgets, in entertainment, business, politics, the arts, the developments in science, and new turns in philosophy. There is not this sense of urgency in the Buddhist view, for though this life can be seen as an opportunity to prepare for a better life when reborn and we must not waste this opportunity, the urgency can be relieved by the reminder that time is, after all, an illusion.

Western senses of time were originally predominantly circular, as in Plato and Aristotle, for example. Then, later the Stoics and the strange early Christian theologian Origen conceived of a strictly repetitive cyclical time; then, Nietzsche still later presents a vision of the eternal return of the very same. But with mainline Christianity the dominant view became linear. Time had a beginning at creation, history had a beginning as Adam and Eve fell from timeless paradise into the on-going toils of life, and, thence history moved on to the birth of the Redeemer and is moving on to the Final Judgment. The Divine drama is linear and finite; it has a beginning, a middle, and an end; and we live some time after the middle on the way to the end. Every moment counts; the tolling bells of clocks tell us every hour that we have one less hour to repent before death and the Last Judgment. Life is serious; it has a purpose.

Kalimpong after monsoon. Photo by the author.

Every moment counts, and historians are ready to depict the passing parade, early on as part of the divine drama, later with cool objectivity. History is a discipline, and even after Hegel, or in reaction to Hegel, historians refrain from pointing to ultimate purposes. There is and was the passing scene with causal entanglements that can be brought out, the Divine drama they leave to theologians. In whatever way the contrast of the sacred and the secular is regarded and debated, the common ground is the linearity of time.

In retrospect I wish I had taken material on Darwinian evolution, at least some of the charts showing some of the sequences. I did give a sketch of the theory and stressed the linearity of time it shows, but I learned later, as we shall see, that the monks were ready to complement that with a counter-story of devolution.

In the logic of scientific method as we saw before, there is a form and purpose to constant research. Science is progressive, ongoing, with no finality; its purpose is to continue. The classic idea that science is climbing toward a final explanation, the ultimate formula like the pinnacle atop a pyramid of knowledge, is giving way to a more modest focus on continuing research itself, like a parade of researchers, not necessarily in step, marching past, not up, the ancient pyramid. However scientific research is pictured, it is just a plain fact that science can explain more today than in earlier times, and there is every reasonable expectation science will be able to explain still more in the years to come. Technology keeps apace, or rather is in partnership. Surely, and thankfully, in medicine and dentistry we see undeniable progress. There is progress; and progress means a linearity of time.

Centuries ago, Indian philosophers addressed the issue between a realist and a positivist view of the atom just as Western philosophers did, much later, after Galileo and Hume. Some argued that minute but unseen entities actually exist, the realist view; while others, more acceptable to Buddhist thought, argued that the notion of an atom was just a way to make sense of a bundle of data, the positivist view. I asked His Holiness if he could see a way to decide this issue, some middle way. He immediately replied in one word, "Research." I saw this as a good example of the way Buddhist thought often deals with a collision of ideas, not by deciding in favor of one or the other, or in trying to see a new idea that may go beyond both, but rather by shifting attention to something else, as the Buddha often did when asked a distracting theoretical question; in this case the shift is to research, not to a new idea, but to an activity. In that activity it is doubtful that either the realist view or the positivist view is prominent in the thought of the researcher; because the focus is on a theory or hypothesis and its empirical verification, the philosophical concerns can come later if at all. With this emphasis on research the notion of a genuine progress is evident at least in the sciences. But does this carry over in the larger picture?

Outside the Christian scenario with a beginning, middle, and an end, in its secular expression there is progress moving toward, well, what? Toward a better world we want to think. But that idea, as Octavio Paz points out, is crumbling. He cites the two world wars, and there are many lesser ones, and "poisoned rivers, forests turned to wastelands, contaminated cities, uninhabited souls. The civilization of abundance is also that of famines in Africa and other places." Paz continues:

Marx's famous phrase about religion as the opiate of the masses can now be applied, and more accurately, to television, which will end up anaesthetizing the human race, sunk in an idiotic beatitude. The future has ceased to be a radiant promise and has become a grim question.[16]

Realistically we could go on to wonder if overall humanity is any better off now than in earlier times. When we regard wars that are more and more lethal. natural disasters like tsunamis, earthquakes, hurricanes, epidemics, and famine, genocide, terrorism, on to pollution and global warming, over-population, poverty, disease, corruption, crime, all the way down to addiction, anxiety, boredom, and empty frivolity, the level of suffering seems constant.

The Buddha said that conditioned life is suffering (*dukkha*), and I wonder if we would get closer to his meaning if we retranslate this, at least at the human level, and say that conditioned life is frustration. In frustration it is easy to see that underlying the distress are the will and desire. It is because we desire or will to have something unattainable or to maintain something passing that we are frustrated. Desire and will are thwarted as opportunities fade, hopes are rendered vain, achievements are nullified, and possessions are lost. All such attempts to cling to what is impermanent frustrate will and desire and create in us a desperate ill will against time and circumstance. The Buddha's way out of *samsara* makes more sense, I would say, to see it as a way out of frustration, for he has us focus on the will and desire as the root of our distress. To say the level of frustration seems constant would make more obvious

---

16   Octavio Paz, *In Light of India*, Harcourt Brace & Company, 1995, p. 194

sense to those who find themselves in comfort and ease, i.e., not suffering, but still anxious about holding onto their advantages. And isn't death the ultimate frustration?

Something like this dark assessment was expressed by His Holiness, more calmly I would say, but just as realistically. We are in an age of decline. As the Hindus have it, we are in the age of Kali, the dark goddess of strife, conflict, and destruction. In class, one of the monks shared the traditional view that in this long decline (we are thinking of eons) we will eventually shrink in size to about three feet in height and have a life span of no more than ten years. His description reminded me of Hobbes' famous description of man in the state of nature, his life "solitary, poor, nasty, brutish, and short."

Kalimpong. Photo by the author.

After this monk brought up what I took to be a fanciful story of our age in decline and our devolution I raised the question of myth versus actuality with His Holiness. I went on in a rather academic way to suggest in what sense myth can be true. The story of Adam and Eve, for example, very vividly conveys the proper relation of human beings to God; in that sense it conveys the truth. To ask then if it is factually true, an actual historical event, is to demean it. If we can see that the story conveyed an important truth, then to say it is or is not factually true, is to miss the point. Myth is more than factual history as music is more than sound waves.

I went on a bit more on fact and fiction, and then His Holiness smiled and gently asked, "The difference?" Of course! We point to actuality as the criterion, and by reference to that we can say myth is merely poetic fancy, not really true, not literally true, a fiction. But what if that very criterion we used, alleged hard fact, is itself an illusion? What then is the criterion? In Buddhist thought fact and fantasy are both in the panoply of illusion; the alleged criterion of brute fact is just part of the passing illusory scene. The question is then, which conveys more aptly its status as illusion and opens us to the ultimate truth it would point to? The answer is easy. Hard fact does not convey its status as illusion, in fact it dissembles, and the more we attend it the more it distracts us from the ultimate truth. Myth is more honest; it presents itself as illusion but one that opens us to the truth.

With this generous view of myth in mind I could appreciate the joy His Holiness showed as he filled me in on more of the myth mentioned by the monk. With restrained smiles like a musician playing Mozart, he told how there had been three earlier Buddhas before the one we revere and that there will be many more, I believe he said twenty-two thousand are yet to come, not only here on earth but throughout the universe. We can expect the next one, Maitreya, when our age of decline reaches its nadir. When, as one monk reported, we have shrunk to a height of about three feet and live only ten years, then a new, much taller Buddha will come. By acts of pure kindness he will show human beings the way to become taller and live longer, eventually to a life span of thousands of years. Perhaps some of His Holiness's smiles came in seeing my reserve, but more obviously he took delight in seeing how truth can be conveyed by stories and myths.

Typically, in myth, in order to free our imagination from the mundane, there is temporal and spatial exaggeration (long, long ago in a place far, far away, etc.), and also exaggerations of power (as in giants and magicians, etc.), and good and evil (as in the saintly and the demonic). Such exaggerations dislodge us from the ordinary, but then the imagination is free for what? Well, let us say it is opened to a truth as expansive as the myth, nay perhaps more in Buddhism, free for timeless, non-perspectival, ultimate truth. Perhaps for different reasons we may all smile a bit now.

His Holiness, with an ease that seems to come to him by nature. is remarkably even-tempered and judicious, but I had noticed also a vivid imagination that he holds under careful control. I was not surprised that, when Erik asked him about his favorite movie, he said it is *Lord of the Rings*. He immediately added, "Perhaps I should not have said that." We both assured him it was in no way indiscreet.

The regard of history, either as the passage of events or the academic discipline, in either case roots us to this world as though it were real. In Buddhist thought, just as the sciences are a distraction from ultimate truth, so too is history a distraction. We wondered why Indian culture, with such a rich history, neglects it, and Indians, both Hindus and Buddhists, could wonder why we take it to be so important. History is worthy to be regarded as relative truth, but the danger is that we take that so seriously to the neglect of what is fundamentally important.

What is fundamentally important is timeless truth, and at a distance from that we are caught in *samsara*, the cycle of suffering, death and rebirth. Just as in a circle, the perimeter with no beginning and no end encircles a central point, so *samsara* encircles the central Truth with every moment on the perimeter at once an end and a beginning endlessly. Just as running along the perimeter of a circle will never get us to the center; so constant regard and fascination with nature and history will never get us to the truth.

We wondered at the start if our linear sense of time and the Buddhist sense of cyclical time could be reconciled. We have seen that there is some common ground in the assessment of the current situation. Our sense of progress is seen as more and more pointless when that toward which we want to see progress is so attenuated, just more episodic sequences of change, each decade with its own style giving way to the next, and so on. The Buddhist sense of an age of decline is hardly brighter even if in eons to come there will be a turn for the better. The cyclical passage of events and a progress to no particular end are not all that different as views of our situation. Is the squirrel running in the squirrel cage in linear or cyclical time? The more things change, the more they stay the same—as pointless progress (hence in what sense progress?) or cyclical repetition.

From the Western point of view this somber view of the current situation needs significant qualification or correction. Is our progress so pointless? A more typical Western voice would point out that there are serious problems to face, and we have the means to deal with some of them, global warming for example. We need to get moving, there are things to do; this is no time for resigned inaction. There is no need to have the ultimate goal all spelled out; leave that to the theologians, philosophers and historians. The immediate problems are obvious enough and need attention now. Let's get on with it. This wholesome reaction has much to be said for it, and in any case it is still a robust attitude maintained in the West.

In contrast, the Karmapa sees an age of decline, and it may be a prevalent view in India. Reports have it that the startling prosperity for a few in the south of India has not diminished the poverty of the majority. How seeing ourselves in an age of decline relieves the urgency of dealing with particular problems here and now I cannot say, but in the larger picture involving eons the sense of urgency is surely diminished. But as His Holiness sees it the decline is inevitable; there is no stopping it, and as with samsara we must accept this as it is in order to move from worldly entanglement toward the freedom of enlightenment.

These large-scale reflections seemed to come to a point one time in our dealing with our cook Dawa. When I first met him as he helped us move into our house, I thought he must be a student, because he was young, nicely dressed, spoke lively English, and was obviously very bright. When I asked him if he was a student, he responded cheerfully, "I am a servant." Just like that.

Indeed, as I mentioned earlier, he was a servant in the household of the Karmapa's parents. He very cheerfully prepared our meals and showed us about the town when we needed something out of the ordinary and was generally helpful. Erik and I knew we would want to leave him some sort of gift, and when he told us he hoped to take a course in computers someday when he had the money, we saw that as just the sort of gift we wanted to make. Moreover, we knew there was a school downtown in Kalimpong that offers suitable courses.

Dawa seemed pleased when we told him that we wanted to give him such a course, but then oddly, as we planned to go to the school together, he showed a curious reluctance. We insisted, though, and the three of us did go down to the school's office, Again, oddly when we had made the arrangements and were ready with the payment, Dawa froze up and could not bring himself to sign the application. I let my mind wonder if this was some hesitation to step beyond his station, some holdover from a very un-Buddhist caste notion, or the disruption of some other pattern. We had heard people say that once a servant always a servant, and here we were urging on a servant the very American notion of educational, social, and economic advancement, or in the current phrase, upward mobility.

Erik was more forthright and dispelled my reflections and ended Dawa'a hesitation by saying firmly, "Dawa, do it." He did sign but still with a continuing unease. It seemed to be social mobility versus social stability, and in the larger contexts, linear and progressive time versus repetitive cyclical time. I am sure it is to his advantage to take the course, or rather I wish I could be sure it is to his advantage even if it is an American-style intrusion. I have to think there can be advancement in a life even if in a hierarchical society in an age of decline. After all, India is a democracy, and the decline is a matter of eons.

We learned four months later that Dawa did indeed finish the course. What possibilities that opened up for him we do not know.

chapter 6
Can there be a meeting of East and West?

When Pythagoras discovered his famous theorem, as the story has it, he made a large sacrifice to Apollo. As well he might, for it was not simply proof of another theorem, but rather it was the discovery of the very ideas of proof and of a theorem; he could *prove* that for *any* right triangle the sum of the squares constructed on the two shorter sides will be equal to the square constructed on the longer side. In ancient times it was well known by surveyors and builders as part of their practical knowledge that a triangle with sides of three, four, and five units is always a right triangle, but Pythagoras went further and showed why that is the case and that the explanation holds for any right triangle; in short, his theorem is universal and necessary. Mathematics as a science was on its way.

His Holiness the 17th Karmapa Trinley Thaye Dorje. Photo by Jachi Shiu.

The startling intellectual clarity that a proof can bring was soon found by Parmenides not only in mathematics but in what we now speak of as ontology, a question of Being, not just beings, entities, or things. Being is; what can be clearer? (Well, it isn't really all that clear, but let's go with the flow.) Then, just as clearly, not-being cannot be. Then, the consequences: plurality cannot be and change cannot be. To have plurality, even if just two, the second would have to be other than Being, hence not-being which in no way can be. Moreover, for change to be, Being would have to become other than Being, hence not-being which in no way can be. This bit of archaic logic had most influential consequences. From the point of view of pure reason, there can be no change and no plurality. This world of many changing things, then, can only be appearance; it is not reality. Of this world there can only be opinion, but not knowledge.

Parmenides' close associate, Zeno, was ready to show that critics of Parmenides who would claim motion certainly does exist fall into paradox. Something like this would be typical: you cannot get to the door, for to go there you must first go half way, to get there you must first go half of that, etc., etc.; hence, in a finite time you cannot take an infinite number of positions, and hence, will never get there. But of course we do get to the door. Zeno hoped to show that an effort to make motion intelligible leads to absurdity; therefore, Parmenides' position stands, strange as it is. Motion, or in general, becoming, is mere appearance and falls short of Being, even if in appearance we do reach the door.

Being and becoming, the intelligible and the sensible, reality and appearance, essence and existence, rationalism and empiricism, *a priori* and *a posteriori*, theory and practice are distinctions that shape much of Western philosophy; and they show more or less vividly the distinction Parmenides opened up.

If we stand back and consider this Being/becoming contrast we may see a promising similarity to Buddhist thought, for in either case Being is time-*less* and stands in contrast to the changing world of appearance or, for Buddhists, illusion. But this similarity immediately opens into a difference, for Parmenides' claim depends on the certainty of pure intellect while the Buddha's depends on non-conceptual ultimate wisdom of pure mind devoid of content. I would see the fork in the road here, East one way, West the other. Parmenides and the Buddha were both active in the sixth century B.C.E., the Buddha some forty years older, but they take the different paths we have seen throughout our discussion.

Can there be common ground, a middle way, between two modes of thought that rely on fundamentally different final appeals? On the one hand, enlightenment goes beyond conceptuality to openness devoid of any vestige of a subject entertaining an object. Short of that there is relative knowledge of appearances that can be and usually are a distraction from the truth. On the other hand, in Western thought intellectual clarity *consists* in conceptuality; beyond that lies mysticism, or more prosaically, nonsense. I doubt that a Hegelian could make a reconciliation of these antithetical modes of thought, and, even if he could, it would be to decide ahead of time in favor of a synthesis, i.e., intellectual clarity. Similarly, I doubt that the wisest Buddhist could try for a middle way without having decided ahead of time that all intellectuality is relative knowledge at best and must fall short of ultimate truth. A stalemate, *stasis*.

Perhaps there can be movement if we note another way to see a final appeal, to authority. During the Middle Ages, the final appeal in assessing a truth claim was Church authority. In modern Western thought going beyond Church authority, the appeal is to cogent argument and in science to coherent theory and empirical evidence. Disciplined reason is the requirement. In Buddhism, the appeal seems similar to the medieval appeal to authority, for the appeal is to an enlightened one, the prime example being the Buddha. His words are final. One does not challenge such a one or respond with an elaborate critique or counter-theory, for all such intellectualizing falls short of ultimate wisdom. One takes the words of the enlightened one as guides on the path to enlightenment. Argument is pointless. This appeal to authority, of course, seems retrograde to modern Western thought.

It is not, however, so simple. There is some similarity between an appeal to ecclesiastical authority and an appeal to an enlightened one, but this similarity is qualified by other considerations. The authority in Buddhism, the final appeal, is, in effect, in each of us, and presumably in all sentient beings. An enlightened one can show the way to that authority, our true self; and in that sense the experienced teacher has something like authority. But each of us can awaken to the ultimate wisdom, the final authority, in the enlightened true self.

I mentioned in class the provocative Zen Buddhist injunction, "If you meet the Buddha, kill the Buddha," and I was surprised that none of the monks had ever heard that, and they were duly puzzled. A Zen master would, of course, remain silent if asked to explain, but not being a Zen master I ventured to suggest that it was to show that looking to another person, even the person of the Buddha, could be a distraction from the way to ultimate truth, for that can only come from within. All external appeals have to be removed. The monks could see that, but to go so far as the Zen master had us imagine they found too troubling for their gentle nature.

Both a Western appeal to reason and ultimate intellectual clarity and an Eastern appeal to true mind and ultimate non-conceptual wisdom, focus on what is thought to be our fundamental nature. But what that is taken to be differs in each case. Socrates would also see that the final authority is within us as his story of prior existence and subsequent recollection shows. Knowledge then is recollection, a re-cognition of our fundamental nature. But that fundamental nature is reason, intellect. We are back to our major theme. If, then, we seek some reconciliation, some middle way between East and West, to what *can* we appeal? We are stymied, in a state of *aporia*.

Let us consider another path, not one toward a final appeal but one in the reverse direction, from enlightenment or, in Socrates' example, a vision of the idea of good, back down to our ordinary world and relative knowledge. We noticed earlier a transition from *sherab* to *yeshe*, from specialized knowledge to ultimate wisdom, but we did not attend the reverse transition. Unless we have achieved *yeshe* we can only speculate on what it is like to have achieved ultimate wisdom and then return to the world of ordinary affairs, but we can see the Buddha as the exemplar. We can be told that this world is illusory, but we do not have assurance of it until we attain true being. Only this gives us a basis from which we can see this ordinary world as not real, as illusion. Given that insight we can regard the world and anyone who comes along with calm but astonishing clarity, as the Buddha shows. We see that to any question the Buddha is open to the inner thoughts of the questioner and responds appropriately to that person to indicate a way from the entanglement in worldly affairs toward freedom and wisdom. Or he sees immediately that the question entangles one in abstractions or in worldly, i.e., illusory concerns that lead nowhere except to further entanglement, and so he responds with silence.

Socrates saw the full implication of his ignorance, or for the positive note, he glimpsed what it is his understanding falls short of, that in virtue of which he is ignorant, the ultimate intelligibility of all things. He then can see the human lot all the more clearly. He can see that our lot is similar to being chained in a cave to guess and argue about shadows and echoes as though they were real. With this clarity on lives led in illusion, Socrates saw his mission and spoke with or questioned his respondents in a way appropriate to them to turn them around toward the sunlight behind them, and perhaps on to ultimate clarity. Or occasionally, he saw that a dialogue with someone would be futile and passed by in silence.

There is a deeper aspect of silence. Even among devotees the teacher must at a certain point fall silent. The Buddha saw that his enlightenment is ineffable, that no amount of talk could convey the achievement. But then he also saw that what he could say might point the way to enlightenment. With practice and more practice a disciple might attain *shunyata*, but for that final achievement the teacher must stand aside in silence. Similarly, Socrates saw that however skillful his talk, his conversant must by his own power come to the essential insight. Socrates brought Meno right up to the critical point, but Meno remained obtuse; he would not reflect on his own rational capacity. Socrates could not give him virtue. Plato could hope for better luck with his readers; as we know, the dialogues typically remain silent on the crucial point: we have to figure it out for ourselves. Teachers know the power of silence.

Do the Buddha and Socrates meet on the return path from clarity and enlightenment in the silence appropriate to the role of teacher?

Early on, His Holiness and I left a question of a pedagogical mission open, but it is appropriate to address it now. His Holiness made it clear that from enlightenment and *nirvana* one could return to this world as anything at all, but I hoped to see how the Buddha not only could but would return as a teacher. It became clear as we explored further aspects of the non-individual and all-inclusive true mind that compassion for all living creatures was essential to it. To stay withdrawn to one's self away from others, as we often imagine a yogi sitting secluded in his cave, could be a means (as it is in advanced Buddhist training) but not an end. Or rather, because the very notion of a private ego is dispelled, notions of a private enlightenment and a private enjoyment of *nirvana* are eradicated. For what is disclosed when the ego, the individual mind, is surpassed in the true mind is at once ultimate wisdom and the commonality of all sentient beings, in a word, compassion. The Buddha saw clearly that he had to show the way to others, and he did just that for the forty-five years he had yet to live.

When I returned home and could explore this issue further I came upon Karen Armstrong's fine book, *Buddha*, in which she addresses this issue directly.[17] She refers to the story in the Pali texts (and she uses the Pali spelling) of Gotama's enlightenment, stories that come with vivid mythic enhancements. When Gotama finally reached enlightenment and the peace of *nirvana*, he was reluctant to go forth to preach, for he saw that enlightenment is ineffable, impossible to explain, and hence no one could understand the way to it. But the god Brahma came down from his heaven and pleaded with the new Buddha saying that many are pining away for lack of this new way and surely some of them will understand. Brahma went on asking the Buddha "to look down at the human race which is drowning in pain and to travel far and wide to save the world."[18] Compassion is given in enlightenment, and an enlightened one cannot dwell in *nirvana* in disregard of other living beings. In realizing that life is suffering, in enlightenment one also

---

17   Karen Armstrong, *Buddha*, Penguin, 2004, pp. 92-97.

18   ibid.p. 95. She refers to Vinaya: Mahavagga, 1:4

realizes compassion, and the Buddha sets out on his mission. Armstrong, rightly I think, takes this story of the Buddha conversing with the god Brahma as a way to represent the Buddha's own thoughts as he entertained the peace of *nirvana* he enjoyed and at the same time the compassion he realized for others. That inner dialogue was concluded as he set forth on his mission. He not only could be the teacher, he *was* the teacher.

Kalimpong. Photo by the author.

In our speculation on the enlightened mind we can see that in the return from the peace of *nirvana* and the freedom of *yeshe*, one can be open to the mundane world of *samsara* as it is and see persons as they are. Those who have gone very far in Tibetan Buddhist thought say something that is startling on first hearing: there is no difference at the ultimate level between *nirvana* and *samsara*. This is very hard for the unenlightened to grasp, but there are impressive symbols that may help. The sitting Buddha is almost always shown in statuary and paintings with his eyes half closed, not in a squint or in sleepiness but in a double vision. He sees this world, and us, from the perspective of his two eyes, and at the same time in an inward vision he is open to non-perspectival, object-less, and subject-less *nirvana*.

We also can see that Socrates would not see a difference between the wisdom of his ignorance showing the need to inquire and his mission barefoot in the marketplace. His highest insight allows him to speak with his respondents skillfully in knowing them better than they know themselves, and thus he hopes to lead them into an intellectual quest.

There are similarities in Socrates' return from his ironic wisdom to his mission in the marketplace and in the Buddha's return from enlightenment to his mission in the ordinary world, but their missions have different aims. They are on different paths.

A typically Western way to approach wisdom is to call basic assumptions into question. For example, Hegel could see his magnificent system summarizing and completing all philosophy in a grand rational synthesis. He saw his philosophy coming to the final expression of what Western philosophers have been groping toward from the beginning. In the unlikely event that he allowed himself to think what could possibly come after his culminating achievement, to be consistent, he would anticipate some antithesis that questions his basic assumptions foreshadowing a yet grander synthesis. If he did he would have been mistaken, for his most innovative critic, Søren Kierkegaard, sees Hegel as a figure of fun. He built a magnificent castle of concepts, but then he had his own individual self, that is certainly not merely a concept, living, as it were, in the humble porter's lodge outside the castle. We see quite a different mode of critique here; humor is not an argument but can be telling. Plato's most severe critic, Friedrich Nietzsche, did not reject Plato's eternal ideas by stressing the temporal realities of actual earthly things but instead shifted attention to what initially brought about such a distinction, a self-denying ascetic will to power. Ludwig Wittgenstein did not engage in the epistemological controversies his own earlier work generated, but in order to open the deepest questions he focused on the language itself that all such philosophy, indeed the whole Western tradition, so often misuses and distorts. Martin Heidegger would call attention to the question of Being that is set aside, especially in science and technology, in our preoccupation and success with beings, the things of the world. Our recent major thinkers, I have mentioned only a few, have shown that we can think outside traditional intellectual confines. It is noteworthy that none of those mentioned offered arguments in the traditional way to establish their positions or would claim that intellectual clarity in the way we have been using it was their aim.

In the last segment of our course, as an example of recent Western philosophy breaking from tradition, we looked at a public address Heidegger gave to a general audience entitled *Memorial Address*. Being for a general audience, it is not the usual heavy Heidegger.[19] There, he contrasts calculative thinking with meditative thinking. By calculative thinking he refers to the thinking about things, beings, that is typical in philosophy and that leads to science and technology. By meditative thinking he does not mean meditative in the Buddhist sense but

---

19 *Discourse on Thinking*, Harper and Row, New York, New York, 1959

what in other places he calls *thinking* as distinct from philosophizing. For example, we can wonder *what* things are and *how* things are as is typical and natural in philosophy and science, but we can on occasion pause and wonder *that* things are.

The first wondering about what and how things are led the Greeks into the philosophy and science so characteristic of subsequent Western thought. In contrast, in wondering *that* things are at all, we step back where there are no guidelines as in calculative thought, no object to focus on, no method to follow, no conceptual scheme to rely on. In a rare freedom we can think in an attentive openness. This thinking is what Heidegger sees as missing in our philosophical efforts.

We wondered earlier from what perspective the significance of science could be viewed, and saw how Descartes traced a metaphysical scheme that would see a subject, a mental substance, attending natural objects, physical substances, with the possibility of knowing them in clear and distinct mathematical ideas. This metaphysical scheme throughout regards objects, substances, i.e., beings, but not Being. Now we see a new viewpoint when we step back from attention to beings, and the science that clarifies them, and let ourselves be open to the question of Being.

Perhaps our major theme, meditation leading toward enlightenment in contrast with disciplined reason leading toward intellectual clarity, should be altered to show that on the Western side what is characteristic is a constant questioning of the tradition, taking it as a stimulus to originality and, perhaps, as an occasion for a major overturning, an adventure of ideas as Alfred North Whitehead speaks of it.

This would stand in contrast to the stable Buddhist tradition wherein any notion of advancement could only be a bringing forth for attention something more of what is already there in Buddhist teaching. This is a process we would call hermeneutic, interpretation in the sense of making more explicit some aspects of what is in the texts already. Nothing new is added. In contrast, in the Western way we would see a history of Buddhist interpretation and reformulation much as we see Christian theology in such a history, another adventure of ideas. Such an adventure is more obvious in the history of science.

When I said something to that effect in an early class, His Holiness and other monks immediately rejected such an idea. Nothing new has been added; it is all in the actual teachings of the Buddha. Occasionally, documents are discovered, purportedly ancient, that express what otherwise would be regarded as an innovation, but being regarded as ancient they could be accepted as part of the original teachings. I could not help thinking of the early mathematicians in the school of Pythagoras who attributed their later advances and innovations not to themselves but to Pythagoras.

There is a deeper reason for the contrast with Western thought. In Buddhism, basic assumptions are not called into question in the Western way because, well, there are none. That sounds odd, but I think it is true to the basis of Buddhist thought— and its stability. At the level of *yeshe* and *non*-conceptual ultimate wisdom there are no assumptions to question, no critiques to assess, no advance to make. Short of *yeshe* there is much sharp questioning and debate among Buddhist philosophers outwardly much like exchanges among Western philosophers. Even so the aim is not primarily toward *intellectual* clarity but more an effort to dispel such logical distractions and clear the path to enlightenment.

We saw that Buddhists could find science and history interesting and could see that they can offer relative truth about the world, but also that they can be distractions. I could tell that His Holiness regarded Western philosophy in the same way but was too tactful to say it. Interesting, especially where we could see similarities, and challenging in a conceptual way, but finally Western philosophy joins science and history as distractions. Toward the end of our sessions I asked His Holiness if he had any questions he would like me to address, and he just smiled and said, "No." I am aware that in Tibetan culture one is taught that it is disrespectful to question teachers, but in our discussions His Holiness felt comfortable in asking questions, so I took his reply as a straightforward response. To a Western teacher his reply could be discouraging, indeed a sign of the teacher's failure; but upon reflection I could see that this is as it should be. Buddhism is not in an adventure of ideas, except as a way to remove obstacles and distractions and then to smooth the way to freedom from *samsara* and, in final fruition, the attainment of enlightenment.

In contrast, Western thought is generated and nurtured by questions, especially by those leading beyond traditional conceptual confines. As the Greeks noted, philosophy begins in wonder. As Socrates said, "This sense of wonder is the mark of the philosopher. Philosophy indeed has no other origin."[20]4 Indeed, this journal is motivated and ordered by questions, and accordingly it hopes to stimulate still more questions.

---

20 *Theaetetus* 155d

Plato shows us how Socrates asked the slave the crucial question that shifted his attention from a hopeless path to an honest inquiry that led to the clarification of the problem. Similarly, Plato contrived his dialogues to stimulate and redirect the readers' inquiry toward a greater intellectual clarity; in short, he hoped to fire the sense of wonder.

Wonder requires openness and may show us a way. The openness allowing us to see and formulate questions in our own tradition also lets us attend other ways of thinking, as here Buddhism. But in a puzzling contrast, Buddhism does not sustain its vitality by incisive questioning of what is fundamental. As we just saw, there is no questioning of basic assumptions in Buddhism because there are none. *Yeshe* is ultimate wisdom that is non-conceptual, and, hence, it is not insight into basic theoretical assumptions. A sharp critical question directed to what is fundamental in Buddhism would be as pointless as aiming an arrow at empty space. But is wonder restricted to questioning fundamental assumptions? The question itself shows that the answer must be no.

Is a meeting of East and West then possible in the openness and wonder that allow our persistent questioning? Let that question hover over some further considerations, but expect to address wonder more explicitly later.

It was mentioned early on that Buddhism is both a philosophy and a religion, but for the most part our discussion concerned mainly the philosophical aspect of Buddhism in conjunction and contrast with Western philosophy. We must notice, however, that seeing Buddhism with a dual aspect is itself a Western imposition. In the West, we distinguish philosophy from religion or philosophy from theology, and we assume such a distinction carries over when we say that Buddhism somehow is both a philosophy and a religion. The challenge, however, is to see Buddhism as a whole beyond that distinction. The challenge is further complicated by the typically Western assumption that a religion focuses on God, or in some times and places, many gods. How could a religion be otherwise? A Buddhist could gently say, "Come see."

A Buddhist shrine or temple is as impressively a spiritual place as cathedrals, churches, temples, or mosques in the West; and the rituals, the costumes, and the ceremonies have many similarities. Moreover, the priestly organizations are similar with a definite hierarchy and usually a spiritual head. A way of life is inculcated and sustained by teachings and practices in Buddhism as well as in the various denominations in the West. The lives of the monks and nuns in each are very similar, and they enjoy similar respect. So, yes, Buddhism is a religion. But the focus is not on a supreme god figure but on the supreme teacher, the one who can show us the way.

All the way through our explorations we hoped that seeing Eastern and Western philosophy in sharp contrast would lead us to see each in clearer light. As it is said, you don't know your homeland well until you leave, adjust to another culture, and then return. The similarities are then highlighted and the differences provocative of a deeper understanding. I see that vividly in the development of a young friend who is a deeply committed Christian and at the same time intensely interested in Buddhism. The contrasts spark brilliant insights that surely would not be forthcoming in a more restricted approach.

Our account has, nevertheless, given little attention to what in a Western way we could call the religious aspects of Buddhism. My mission, if I may put it so, was philosophical and pedagogical. Or, to put it another way, as I did at the beginning, I did not see it as a spiritual quest. What drew me were the philosophical issues Eastern and Western that we have considered in this account. Discussion with the Karmapa as we tried to clarify the issues was reward enough for me. Accordingly, we explored the more strictly religious issue only incidentally.

The doctrine of rebirth is an example of what I have in mind as a religious issue. In discussing David Hume in conjunction with the Buddhist notion of the self, I tried to show how a Westerner might see that a sequence of birth, life, death, and rebirth is possible. That possibility came with a non-substantial conception of the self that both Buddhists and Hume maintain. As the Karmapa said, the self is a mind stream, and that, as I understood it, could continue after the death event. But the plausibility, or perhaps I should say, the believability of such a sequence of death and rebirth is another matter.

What stands against it, as this Westerner sees it, is the undisguised recognition that one's *individual* life abruptly ends. That thought, our eventual not-being here, is at once so empty, and thereby so overwhelming, that we typically and constantly distract ourselves from it. The thought of one's no longer being here gives a person nothing to focus on, so the imagination supplies a distraction, a cover-up, anything to disguise or fill the void. Faith that there is something more for an individual after death, to be genuine, must be *subsequent* to that stark recognition of one's finitude. I must say, not proudly but candidly, that I cannot make such a leap of faith. Without such a leap I cannot see a picture showing a sequence of birth, death, and rebirth as anything but distraction.

Let me put this in another way. Animals perceive, but are they aware *that* they perceive? I think not. The awareness we have, however, includes awareness that it is awareness. Moreover, this *reflexive* awareness we have is open to the awareness that it faces its own death, and it is that awareness of its own not-being that takes so much courage to accept. A picture of a life going on after death is much more attractive and makes an enthralling distraction.

Kalimpong. Photo by the author.

As we noted, the Karmapa saw Western philosophy, science, and history as interesting but finally as distractions from the ultimate truth; and here I see an Eastern doctrine of rebirth as interesting but finally as a distraction from thinking of one's individual death without disguise. Clearly, the individuality of death that

I am maintaining here, as that from which we constantly distract ourselves, is a Western emphasis. It does not depend on a return to a notion of a substantial self, however. The finite reflexive consciousness is where we begin and where we end.

Such a notion stands in contrast to the Buddhist view. There, distraction is not from the finitude of reflexive consciousness, a self recognizing its own death, but the distraction is from the non-individual Buddha mind. As we turn to temporal matters and, by extension, concern for science, history, and Western philosophy, we turn ourselves from our true mind, the Buddha mind. Both modes of thought see distractions, but then there is the difference: distraction from one's individual death, distraction from the non-individual Buddha mind.

Let us look more closely at the inevitable common denominator of us all, the concern all human beings have whatever their religious or philosophical orientation: Death. We all meet there somehow. Does this meeting point of all human beings show us another way?

To accept that there is a rebirth after death in the on-going *samsara* takes something like faith, as we mentioned above, but that is not the deepest regard of death in Buddhism. The true way is given in the ultimate truth when the individual self becomes its true self, the Buddha mind, and that is non-individual, timeless, devoid of any subject regarding any object, and—here is the point we need to see—it is also devoid of such sequential contrasts as life/death. The question, "Is there life after death?" is surpassed, as any sequence of before and after is erased.

Or not. If not, one falls short of truth, remains in *samsara* and sees death as a transition, a *bardo*, into yet another life fraught with frustration and then death and so on. Tibetans trace out in elaborate details the various stages of this *bardo* from death into another life. With sufficient meditative practice and success, one can surpass this temporal sequence.

We noted earlier that Socrates said philosophy is "practicing dying" meaning that in the quest for intellectual clarity we must try to think as though disembodied or, to put it less dramatically, we must think objectively. In contrast Plato puts it very dramatically in his description of Socrates' death. In the death scene we see that Socrates not only does not fear death he welcomes it. Death frees him from the distractions of the bodily senses and passions and gives him the freedom to see clearly what he had been seeking in his life-long quest. What the court that condemned him and the jailer who brought the cup regarded as poison he took as medicine (*pharmakon* can mean either) that will cure him of his entanglement in bodily and worldly matters. The Karmapa smiled as he immediately saw a parallel with Buddhist practice in meditation, but we did not follow that up, for the bell rang, and the Karmapa had other obligations.

As Socrates would have us see, at death after a philosophic life, that is, a life well practiced in dying, a person becomes non-individualized pure intellect. If we say instead that we become pure mind, or better yet if we can say we become the Buddha Mind, we can also smile; for we seem to be on the same path. The soul in timeless impersonal immortality reaches its true nature. It is true that toward the end of the *Phaedo*, Plato has Socrates offer an elaborate myth depicting individual souls in a story of birth, death, and rebirth; but the force of the argument and the subsequent death scene present the deeper Socratic message: at death we are freed from the world and individuality and freed to the all inclusive intelligibility that motivated Socrates' quest. There is more than a parallel here with Buddhism; indeed, there appears a genuine convergence.

Earlier the notion that at death Socrates became pure intellect led me to ask His Holiness if in enlightenment one becomes *dharma*, and he was intrigued and gave a cautious but tentative assent. And well he should be cautious, for we are at the edge of understanding, Western or Eastern. Is the *dharma* coalescent with the over-arching intelligibility expressed in Plato's idea of good? Is that the pattern of active mind as His Holiness might put it? That is indeed an intriguing thought and deserves careful reflection.

It is an attractive idea, but no, ultimate wisdom is devoid of pattern. *Dharma* then is the way to ultimate wisdom, a path not a destination, or it is the doctrine presenting the way. Khenpo Tsering told me that the root meaning of *dharma* is cleansing, and hence it is a means to the end, pure mind. It is not the pattern of pure mind, as my Western mind hoped.

Important as Plato is in shaping Western philosophy, his notion that it is a non-individual soul that is immortal is not carried into the mainstream of Western thought. The dominant view is quite different. It sees an individual soul in the face of the ultimate individual, God. This relation of the self to God, one self to another Self, is the most fundamental and the most important relation, for life after death whether bliss in heaven or torment in hell depends on the purity of this relation. It defines us and shapes our destiny. But in Plotinus and then in Christian mysticism in which one dissolves individuality in merging into a union with ineffable God, and in negative theology according to which we can only say what God is not, that God is no-thing, any notion of God as an individual entity, however perfect, is superseded, as is the notion of the individual soul in its final enlightenment. The convergence with Buddhism we just noted seems virtually realized.

This segment of Western thought, regarding mystical union with the ineffable God and the notion of God as no-thing is, however, at odds with the mainstream of Western thought much as Buddhism is, and it presents our main problem anew. Western thought for the most part still focuses on the individual, both divine and human, and secular thought focuses on the individuality of persons, their political rights, education, well-being, and achievements. And there is the stunning success of the sciences that focus on particular entities ranging from galaxies to quarks. It is doubtful that Christian mysticism and negative theology will become mainstream any time soon.

The mainstream Western focus on individuality shows death as one's very own, not an attainment of non-individual Buddha mind or non-individual pure intellect but a terminus of one's own self. In the face of this stark recognition one can then face the challenge of faith, at this level a genuine faith in the miracle of an eternal life of the immortal individual soul after death. Such a faith has life-changing force and reward as Christianity and Islam have shown through the centuries.

Faith in individual immortality is, of course, in sharp contrast with Buddhist thought that also has endured through the centuries. There is the common denominator of death, but how it is regarded in

Buddhism and how it is regarded in mainstream Western thought show a fundamental difference once again.

So far the paths we have followed in a quest for a meeting of East and West, both those dealing with broad philosophical issues and those dealing with personal concerns, have shown some similarities in thought, but each time we saw that the similarities open into difference. Is there yet another way?

Yes. We saw an example earlier. In the face of two intellectual alternatives standing in conflict, a realist interpretation of the theory of the atom or a positivist interpretation, the Karmapa shifted attention away from the conflicting concepts to an *activity*, actual research. Now a similar shift of attention to an activity may show another path.

As we actively entertained the larger issues of thought, Eastern and Western, were we not on a middle way all along? In our discussions it was good will and an open mind that sustained our explorations, and now we need to focus on that rapport underlying our actual discussion. Neither good will nor open-mindedness was an explicit topic to discuss, but they were silently exemplified and maintained as they sustained our discussion. Now, we need to shift our attention to that activity, what was actually going on. In that rapport we are and have been on a middle way throughout our explorations, for when we look at our actual situation and what we are doing, there is a meeting of minds in our honest discussion. In some cases it is an agreement to disagree, but even so an abiding good will prevails in that agreement.

The old Greek injunction, *Know Thyself*, is especially apt here. I have rarely known a person old or young who had the ease and self-honesty apparent in the Karmapa. Even though in his position there can be temptations, there is not the slightest hint of selfishness, arrogance, pretense, vanity, or condescension in his nature. It is not that he resists them; rather, they are just not there to be resisted. With such self-lucidity as a basis he can meet others with unqualified good will.

Immanuel Kant began his best known book on ethics this way: "Nothing in the world—indeed nothing even beyond the world—can possibly be conceived which could be called good without qualification except a GOOD WILL."[21] We can understand his statement at the conversational level, but, of course, Kant had deeper thoughts in mind. Let us look at his powerful but complex moral philosophy just enough for us to see his treatment of good will and to highlight its difference from the Buddhist position but also its compatibility.

For Kant, practical reason is at the heart of the matter. It is by theoretical reason that we come to knowledge, but it is by practical reason that we initiate action. Kant sees will and practical reason as the same. As moral agents we initiate action guided by a principle of action, and if that principle is consistent, i.e., can hold universally, action in accordance with it is moral and stems from a good will. For a counter-example, there is a rational way to rob a bank, but that principle of action is inconsistent. For a principle is universal, and if the principle guiding the robbing of the bank, taking something against the will of another, were universal, the robber would be willing against his own will in willing that someone take something   against his will.

---

21 *Foundations of the Metaphysics of Morals* 393, Lewis White Beck trans. Macmillan Publishing Company, New York, 1990

A person of good will always wills in accordance with a principle that he or she can will to be universal. The universality of principle is the final appeal.

Flag of the 16th Karmapa. Photo by the author.

Now here is the point we need to see. In respecting one's own reason, one in effect respects all rational agents. Kant puts the second formulation of his famous categorical imperative this way: "Act so that you treat humanity, whether in your own person or in that of another, always as an end and never as a means only."[22] When Kant said that good will is the only unqualifiedly good thing, he meant a will acting out of a respect for the practical reason that we all share; its form is a universality independent of individual empirical selves and their own wants and desires. As rational agents we have a basis for respecting other rational agents; we see them as ends in themselves worthy of the respect we have for our own reason. In so acting we show our good will.

In the Buddhist mode, compassion is recognition of the non-individual Buddha nature we (and all sentient beings) share. Compassion has its basis in this commonality. For Kant it is the commonality of reason that all rational agents share and is the basis of good will. Both compassion and good will are recognized as our true non-egoistic nature, but one is based on the Buddha mind and the other on reason. We are back to our familiar contrast. But is wonder so divided?

Earlier, we noticed that we can see our Western theoretical orientation all the more clearly as it contrasts with the Eastern meditative orientation, and vice versa, but we did not go on to explore what our standpoint had to be in order for us to entertain that contrast. That standpoint cannot be exclusively theoretical or exclusively meditative if we hold both modes of thought in contrast.

We noticed that in dealing with the *cogito*, the monks saw an occasion for humor as they entertained the contrast of the Cartesian context with the Buddhist

---

22   ibid.429

context, and I found that encouraging because they had to have some understanding of both to enjoy the humor. Now, in giving our attention to the much larger contrast of Eastern and Western thought in general, we need not see an occasion for humor, but we do enjoy the freedom and openness that the Greeks would speak of as wonder. In an occasion for laughter there is a kind of free-fall, because we are free from an initial context and are not quite in another, and in that freedom we can appreciate the final absurdity of the conjunction of the two contexts. Similarly, here in wonder we have to step back from the security of our own traditional mode of thought but find ourselves not yet secure in another. In entertaining the contrast we are in a kind of suspension, if not a free-fall, that can be exhilarating. We are in wonder.

At the start we did wonder from what standpoint we could regard our major theme contrasting Eastern and Western thought, but thereafter all the way through we kept our eye on the two modes in contrast. Now, we are shifting our attention and notice we elaborated the theme from a position of wonder that was neither explicitly intellectual nor meditative. Such freedom can be exhilarating, but not because we are in suspension and ready for laughter, but because we interact with one another in the freedom of good will and the openness of compassion. Are we beyond *stasis*, stalemate, and beyond being stymied, *aporia*? Yes. We can see and did see an opportunity for movement: actual interaction, actual inquiry beyond *stasis* and an openness beyond *aporia*.

In our explorations and inquiries it was obvious that His Holiness and I had an appreciation of both Eastern and Western modes of thought, and we were most congenial as we addressed the issues and were stimulated by the puzzles. The major difference of East and West was recognized, but there was an appreciation and respect from both sides providing a middle way that happily came with many smiles if not laughter. Perhaps we can see now that it is wonder that joins us in the compassion and good will shown in our explorations. Or the other way also: Good will and compassion allow a joint inquiry that wonder has opened. It is that conjunction and activity that shows an actual meeting of East and West. We are in ourselves as inquirers a meeting of East and West, and the reader who has come this far is on this middle way with us.

We are all born into ignorance, and by nature we are all opened into wonder.

A journal as a report can come to an end; thoughts and reflections continue. People working in philosophy in the Western way often imagine what shrewd old Socrates would say of their efforts, and imagining his critical and probing questions sharpens many a thought. An encounter with the Buddha has a similar effect. "What would the Buddha think?" is a question that always deepens one's reflections, not only while dealing with philosophical issues, but also at the various turns in everyday life. We live facing contingencies and the questions they generate, and the deeper the questions the more open are our minds and, perhaps, the more likely we are to gain some illumination.

In our opening sentence we had it refer back to itself, and here as we conclude we can see we have turned our thoughts back to the activity we have been engaged in and the wonder that opened it. In this way a journal presenting the actual engagement of two open minds and the good will sustaining both has an advantage over a necessarily more detached *treatise*.

Initially, I decided on a philosophical *journal* as a way to make challenging philosophical thoughts more accessible to the general reader, for in focusing on the actual exchanges between His Holiness and me the journal could be more vivid and at the same time all the more easily indicate deeper aspects of the contrast of Eastern and Western thought. But further reflection showed that it was precisely that personal engagement that needed to be focused on to enlighten what otherwise would have been our familiar intellectual impasse, *stasis* and *aporia* yet again. There was an actual middle way. The journal initially decided on as appropriate rhetoric became itself thematic.

Was the philosophical engagement any more Western than Eastern or Eastern than Western? I hope we can see that the answer can be seen in the asking.

Here at the end let us hear some words of the teachers. After remarking that there are not many things he can confidently assert, Socrates goes on to say:

> . . . [T]he belief in the duty of inquiring after what we do not know will make us better and braver and less helpless than the notion that there is not even a possibility of discovering what we do not know, nor any duty of inquiring after it—this is a point for which I am determined to do battle, so far as I am able, both in word and deed.[23]

The Buddha said:

---

23 *Meno* 86b-c, ibid.

O monks, just as a goldsmith tests his gold by melting, cutting, and rubbing (on a touchstone), sages accept my teachings after full examination, and not just out of devotion.[24]

Monks making prostrations towards the Bodhi Tree at Bodh Gaya. Photo by the author.

24 The Tattvasamgraha

Afterword

a dialogue

I have been hearing derisive laughter in the background and it is quite puzzling. Perhaps you have been hearing it also. Ah, here he comes. It is John Smith. I am sure you also know him.

HARRISON J. PEMBERTON:
So, John, what do you have to say to us?

JOHN SMITH:
I'll be blunt and just say your question—can there be a meeting of East and West?—is pointless. Yes, laughable. There is a meeting, as everyone knows, in technology. You told me the other day you had a splendid student, a major in philosophy and Chinese, who applied for a Fulbright to China. You thought that with his grades and fluency in Chinese—indeed he reads Lao-tzu with

ease—that he had an excellent chance. He was rejected. You told me word came back that the Chinese were not interested in old sages, no; they want applicants well-schooled in technology. There is the pertinent word again: technology. Everyone knows that today technology shapes human lives globally, and that technological research and manufacture thrive in Japan, South Korea, India, and now China as well as in the West. So a meeting? No, rather a merger. So now where is your big question?

HARRISON J. PEMBERTON:
Well, John, what you say is obvious enough, but what I had in mind goes deeper—if I may put it so. Buddhism culminating in enlightenment and Western thought maintaining the pursuit of rational clarity remain distinctly apart. There is no merger at that level. So we do not yet have a meeting of East and West. But now it was from that difference that we moved to questioning, inquiry, examining. Think carefully now of the position one takes in such questioning. In questioning there is a stepping back into a freedom from both but an awareness of both as incompatible. Can you see a three-part scheme here of East, West, and your stepping back to a position from which you see them in contrast? Now let the Buddha and Socrates step back and join in that freedom of inquiry. Each in this freedom moving from their own mode of thought to the other and seeing the incompatability, wouldn't they then, yes, wouldn't they then join in wholesome and hearty laughter? We saw earlier that thinking along one line of thought, then being triggered to another that is incompatible, is often the occasion for laughter. Let us then enjoy their

laughter. Perhaps we can join them in our own regard of East and West. Now, John, can you join us in a laugh at this level?

John Smith:
Yeah, yeah.

—Harrison J. Pemberton, August 2013

Index

A

active mind 38, 40, 115
aesthetic continuum 76
aporia 27, 99, 121, 123
Aristotle 16, 33, 52, 59
awareness 24, 126

B

Birth of Tragedy, The 55, 56
black holes 61, 62
Bodh Gaya 124
Bodhi Tree 124
Buddha nature 24, 32, 120

C

capitalism 82

G

Galileo 59, 60, 86
geometry 29, 31, 33, 58, 78
God 39, 44, 46, 51, 52, 57, 58, 89, 110, 115, 116
good will 12, 117, 118, 119, 120, 121, 122, 123

H

Hegel, Georg Wilhelm Friedrich 19, 82, 85, 104
Heidegger, Martin 19, 105, 106
Hobbes, Thomas 88
Hume, David 19, 39, 70, 71, 72, 73, 74, 75, 79, 80, 86, 111
humor 9, 50, 51, 105, 120, 121

I

illusion 36, 46, 47, 48, 56, 59, 62, 65, 66, 83, 89, 97, 100
individualism 52, 53
inquiry 17, 18, 28, 52, 56, 57, 109, 121, 122, 126
irony 23, 56

J

journal 3, 5, 3, 108, 122, 123

K

Kalimpong 3, 5, 6, 7, 9, 10, 11, 14, 15, 18, 19, 21, 47, 61, 70, 77, 84, 88, 93, 103, 112, 131
Kant, Immanuel 63, 64, 65, 66, 67, 118, 119, 120
Karmapa Trinley Thaye Dorje 7, 9, 10, 16, 49, 96
Kierkegaard, Søren 104
King Midas 56

L

linear time 22, 82, 83
Locke, John 52, 53
Lord of the Rings 90

M

Mahabodhi temple 19
Mahakala puja 79
Mahayana Buddhism 70
Marx, Karl 19, 82, 87
meditation 4, 13, 14, 22, 36, 38, 49, 50, 79, 106, 114
Meno 19, 23, 26, 27, 28, 29, 42, 101, 123
Meno's puzzle (toothpicks) 26
mens sive animus 46
middle way 86, 97, 98, 99, 117, 122, 123
Millay, Edna St. Vincent 34
mind 7, 17, 18, 22, 23, 24, 26, 29, 30, 33, 37, 38, 39, 40, 41, 42,
46, 47, 48, 49, 50, 51, 52, 53, 57, 58, 59, 62, 66, 72, 73, 74, 78, 89,
93, 97, 99, 101, 102, 103, 111, 113, 114, 115, 116, 117, 118, 120, 126
monsoon 6, 12, 29, 30, 84
Mozart, Wolfgang Amadeus 89
myth 89, 90, 114

N

Newton, Sir Isaac 34, 35
Nietzsche, Friedrich 55, 56, 66, 67, 84, 105
nirvana 43, 101, 102, 103, 104
Northrop, F.S.C. 76

O

Origen 84

Publishing finished
in January 2022 by Pulsio
Publisher Number: 4014
Legal Deposit: January 2022
Printed in Bulgaria